#TheStoriesWeTell

To Mom. I love you.

the. stories we tell

Shift your story
Shift your sh#t

JUANENE FRYDMAN

First published in 2020 by Juanene Frydman

ISBN: 978-0-6398025-6-5 (print)

Also available as an ebook.

Copy edited by Tracey Hawthorne
Illustrations by Rob Hooper
Cover design by Rob Hooper
Typesetting by Book Lingo
eBook Conversion by Book Lingo

"A beautifully written and insightful book that provides a framework for unlocking that 'Aha' moment to find out exactly who you really are. Juanene lays out the context of the Enneagram in a way that is easy to understand as well as what this means to how you can live an even more fulfilled life."
Tessa Graham — International Consultant and Collaborator

"Enneagram de-mystified at last! Brilliant way to understand the stories that trip us all up. Juanene has the knack of synthesising her immense understanding of the complex enneagram and making it user friendly! I love the way she helps you 'befriend' your animal type with deeply insightful questions alongside very practical tips."
Kate Emmerson — International author, speaker and retreat leader

"Discovering my own type brought the realisation that I can't play effectively with others until I understand my own story. I would recommend this book to both parents and people in the privileged position of leading and nurturing others."
Brenda Matyolo — Parent and COO of African Rainbow Capital

"I had been introduced to my Enneagram type through Juanene a few years ago and found this concept to be insightful and intuitive. Making the links to the animal types is very relatable, brings life and expresses the character of the Enneagram types so accurately. J, because of her deep expertise with the Enneagram, articulates and expresses this so effortlessly in this book. She creates intrigue and fascination, leaving one enticed and wanting to explore your animal type even deeper."
Paulette Daniels — Executive Head of Human Capital, Sanlam Sky (Retail Mass)

"The inscription to this book is simple enough: 'To Mom. I love you.' But Juanene's brave introduction shows how that simple message is a point on a journey of seeking a mother's love as the foundation for feeling good enough. This is a book about the stories that run our lives and the lenses through which we see what we call reality. Using the Enneagram as her base, Juanene shows us a way to become conscious of the stories that tell us and, most importantly, how we can reframe those stories. If you'd like to choose your story instead of being chosen by it, read this book."

Orenna Krut — Managing Director, Troupant Publishers

"We all have stories to tell but Juanene's earliest memories are powerful and memorable. Her pain of unrequited love and a constant searching for answers led her to the Enneagram and an awakening of the true Juanene. This book is far more than 'good enough', it is a fantastic insight into beliefs, habits and behaviors. It is the only book you need to read to help to understand and make sense of your own personal story. It will change you forever!"

Sue Brooks — CEO and Founder of Freestone Group

"This book has truly inspired me to trust the process of personal growth. Juanene has a unique way of illustrating how the gentle combination of blending our minds, hearts and bodies enable a fresh view of the world and give us hope for a lifetime of lifelong, joyous learning and loving."

Catherine Young — Founder of Thinkroom

"Being an Owl, I love information that is clear, direct and practical. #TheStoriesWeTell provides all of that as well as giving deep insights into what 'runs' us and how we can grow into the best version of ourselves. The personal stories make it highly relatable and reminds us that below all our ego constructs we are deeply connected to one another."

Dr Loretta Ferrucci — Registered homeopath

"Looking for self enlightenment? It starts internally in our deepest recesses, the place we seldom delve into. Now is the time to turn to #TheStoriesWeTell and let Juanene light the path to your inner playbook and decode your greatest challenges and ultimate freedom."
Brett Preston — CEO Mirari Group

"Juanene has created a wonderfully creative and descriptive resource for all those wanting to understand their inner stories and how they define their view on the world, relationships and life. She does this through sharing some beautifully written stories of her own life to make it 'real'. She has also masterfully crafted animal characters and analogies to help make this age old wisdom of the Enneagram stick. Delving into this work is transformational and this book will help you on your journey towards being your best self."
Debbie Craig — Founder & MD of Catalyst Consulting, Author of PowerUp8

"I can attest to the great value that this book, Juanene Frydman, fondly known as J, has gifted the world. The well-written, clever, accessible way in the manner Juanene portrays each of us in a non-judgemental and self-explorative curious way – whether you are the CEO of a large Fortune500 company or a person seeking personal improvement in your own private capacity – ignites the spark to self-discovery, self-mastery and promoting a healthier world. Juanene's fundamental principles of integrity, honesty and ethics are evident in the book allowing her readers to give permission to do the same. In deep gratitude for her relentless commitment throughout her years as an international executive and personal coach to be a change-maker and transformational shape-shifter, and quantifying her learnings in her teachings in this book."
Joanna Kleovoulou — Clinical Psychologist and Founder of PsychMatters Centre

"Juanene refers to it as 'asking yourself what you're running from.' I hate Sundays. They're too slow. I have to be on the go. Constantly. But her question got me to stop. This book is a must read, you will understand so much more about yourself and it will provide you with very practical mechanisms to be more aware of your triggers and how to cope better."

Lynette Armstrong — Acting Managing Director of Debswana Diamond Company

Mind is the Master power that moulds and makes,
And Man is Mind, and evermore he takes
The tool of Thought, and, shaping what he wills,
Brings forth a thousand joys, a thousand ills: –
He thinks in secret, and it comes to pass:
Environment is but his looking-glass

– From 'As a Man Thinketh' (1902) by James Allen

Contents

Foreword

As Socrates famously said, "the unexamined life is not worth living". Thus the well-known Ancient Greek aphorism "Know Thyself" has echoed through the ages. It urges us to reflect inward to reach a measure of self-awareness, an endeavour which will assist us in living to our full potential and attaining a modicum of contentment. In our pursuit of happiness, it is prudent to consider the wisdom within the mystical writings of the Upanishads, which tell us that "it would be easier to roll up the entire sky into a small cloth than it would be to obtain true happiness without knowing the self." And how do we go about discovering the self? To be sure, there are many tools which can enlighten the way to a deeper self-knowledge, but I have found the archetypal framework of the Enneagram to be a powerful source of wisdom, which can help us in our journey inward. In this enlightening book, Juanene has woven the Enneagram into a unique narrative of self-discovery to help you shift your inner story to one of self-love and empowerment.

The Enneagram changed my life too almost 21 years ago when I encountered Sister Doris Gastonguay on a friend's patio in Lilongwe, Malawi, where we lived for 16 years. Sister Doris opened a door for me which has led to a vocation of learning and teaching the Enneagram across the globe. The difference I have seen it make in people's lives has been most gratifying and it spurs me on to continue to reveal its potential for positive change. I received another great gift from Malawi: it was the first time I had lived in a country other than my native South Africa, one with a diverse community, a beautifully varied culture and singular spiritual traditions, which taught me that there are different ways of being in the world.

The Enneagram gave me a map to negotiate and embrace

these differences. For the first time, I began to understand why we think, feel and act the way we do, and why we often struggle to get along. The nine personalities of the Enneagram made perfect sense to me and I felt that, at last, my questioning had a structure and direction which had been missing for so long.

From birth we start writing our own life stories. Who we become is shaped by how we perceive the world through our senses. Each experience forms the different facets of our reality, our place in it and our perception of the self in relation to this personal truth as we see it. We are all born with a set of qualities which we develop, shape, distort, suppress – or which go unrecognised through lack of self-awareness. We often cannot see the inherent qualities in ourselves and others due to the filters and beliefs we acquire along the way. Our stories keep us captive and we hook into a one-dimensional way of seeing things. Unconsciously we become prisoners of our perceptions.

The Enneagram is an instrument with which we can shatter our misguided notions of the self and delve deeper into Socrates' imperative of examining life as we know it to arrive at the untold insights that await us. The depth of my relationship with others and the world depends on how well I know myself. I cannot know you or the world better than I know myself. The process of self-discovery is a never-ending opportunity to see yourself and others through new eyes. As we journey further into life, we are invited to go deeper into the very core of our being. Embarking on an examined life through the Enneagram is not about changing who you are, but about discovering all the distinct aspects of yourself. This self-knowledge leads us to respect and honour ourselves and each other. Once we become aware of the self, we realize that we all share in the same condition in uniquely different ways.

Teaching the Enneagram over the last 20 years, I have seen so many people releasing the weight of a life lived in half measures, and realising for the first time that what stands between me and others is myself. I am the reason for my own unhappiness. What changed me deeply is the realisation that the Enneagram is not just another personality system; it's a roadmap to awakening the giant within each one of us, awakening our own true nature and moving toward wholeness. We are all searching, although we might not consciously be aware of it; we are searching for love in our relationships, happiness in everyday life experiences and peace within ourselves and the world.

Juanene's book provides an opportunity for you to discover the Enneagram and how it can show you a different way of being. She is an internationally recognized executive coach and facilitator, and now author. Her passion has always been that of storytelling and the power of the inner narrative. She speaks of how her life was forever changed in 2013 when she fell upon the Enneagram, became aware of her own narrative and came to profound insights. She invites us to look at our own life stories, to become aware of the "undercurrents" of our own stories and to break free from the "triggers" that push us to revert to our old patterns. Such is the impact of this change in her life that Juanene has taken to writing this book to empower you to recognize the stories you tell and how these stories quietly yet determinedly impact on your behaviour, moods and emotions. The pages of this book will not only aid you in the discovery of your story, but will give you practical tools that will support you in your path toward personal mastery.

This book is for you if you are interested in the process of self-knowledge and intend to use your talents to "be the change that you wish to see in the world". As Rilke once said, "go into yourself and see how deep the place is from which your life flows".

Suzette Fischer
Spiritual Director and Training Associate of the Narrative Enneagram in South Africa

INTRODUCTION

My story and how it shaped me

'The neural networks formed while in our mother's womb and during childhood are the foundation for our later beliefs. They are the beliefs we carry into adulthood and through which we understand and interpret our experiences. And while the first lessons from our infancy generally serve us well, they can negatively colour future experiences that would otherwise have been perceived as benign or even positive.'

from Power Up Your Brain *by David Perlmutter and Alberto Villoldo*

I believe that both nature and nurture impact on who we are and who we become. The way we're raised has a definite effect on determining the personality we show to the world.

I also believe that we're exposed to nine core internal narratives during our formative years, based on what we see and hear, and, more importantly, on the actions we take and the results of those actions. These narratives are our stories, and while we all have all nine, there's usually one that's more dominant than the rest. This is what I call our internal story.

Because of the hardwiring of our brains we tend, the older we get and the less aware we become, to lean more into what's known as 'negativity bias'. This is, according to psychologists, our tendency to give more attention to negative stimuli in our lives than positive, for example, we remember criticism better than praise, or we focus on how much of our time we give to others and their needs, and how little we receive in return.

Because of this, we become more in tune with the unhealthy aspect of our inner stories, which in turn impacts our behaviour, our emotions and the thoughts we hold of ourselves and others.

For example, we may fall into a story of martyrdom and hold a sense of resentment towards others, or focus our attention on how no one loves us in spite of how much we do for them.

This gap between what we give and what we receive is what we focus on, instead of looking for where we're loved and, more importantly, at how we can love ourselves instead of waiting for love to be given to us in exchange for something we've said or done.

Another example: let's say that your story is that in order to be loved, you have to love first – a give-to-get exchange. You'll have learned this as a child: you might have observed an adult in your family demonstrating this behaviour, or have learned that by being the loving child, you received the love you so wanted and needed.

The 'healthy' version of this inner story is your knowing that in order to be loved, you do not have to put other people and their needs ahead of your own, that your needs can come first. It's also knowing that you're worthy of being loved just because of who you are and not because of what you give to others.

The 'unhealthy' version – what I call the 'shadow' side – is that you allow yourself to be taken for granted and you might even resort to manipulation to ensure that your need for love is met.

Finding the story that runs our life isn't easy. Most often it's hidden from us, not because we don't know it – to the contrary, it's become so known to us that we live with it as a part of us that can't be changed. It's a little like having a niggling pain in our body and, because it isn't hampering our day-to-day living, we move ahead in life and soon we forget it's even there.

My own story is 'I'm not good enough'. I fell upon it the hard way, and only in my late 40s. Before that it was totally hidden from me. I didn't understand that it drove my every decision, my relationships, my parenting, my career. As an adult, I thought I was simply living my life. I didn't realise that in every action I took, I was trying to prove to myself that I was good enough. Even when the world shouted at me, 'You are good enough!' I never believed it; all I did was try harder to be 'good-er', closer to perfect and correct, more good enough.

All this changed in 2013, when I stood beside my mother's hospital bed as she lay dying. My mom, aged 68, had been diagnosed with cancer in December 2012; three months later, we were told to say our goodbyes. 'She's slipping away fast,' the doctor said. 'She can hear you, though, so say what needs to be said.'

But, for me, it was less about what I needed to say than what I so wanted to hear.

My mother had never told me that she loved me – I'd never once heard her say those words. And only once had I said 'I love you' to her, just before my 40th birthday – and I only did so because of a process in a personal-transformation workshop I was attending at the time. We were told to tell someone significant in our lives that we loved them and risk them not saying it in reply. Her response? She laughed, and said, 'I know you love me. You didn't have to put yourself through this.'

That omission had stretched over a lifetime. It was an exclusion that became, for me, a deeply held story, and which pulled the strings of my life and behaviour like a puppeteer – but quietly, without my noticing, for a very long time.

So those were the only three words on my mind that night, standing by her hospital bed: the three words I most wanted to hear from her. Leaning forward, I whispered in her ear, 'Mom, I love you.'

She heard me. I know she heard me. Her hands, agitated before, became calmer, and her body stilled. But she remained silent.

The doctor approached, moving towards one of the monitors and turning it away from me. I realised then that the monitors were quiet. Mom had begun her new journey.

A howl arose from the deepest, darkest corners of my being, travelling up a blackened path, gathering momentum as it moved through my body until it reached my mouth. It spewed out in a guttural cry of pain. Mom was gone. And she'd died never having said those words to me.

I was 48 years old, a grown woman and a mother myself. I was crippled with emotional pain. My quest to make my mom love me was over. What was I to do?

I was an international executive coach. I worked with leaders all over the world, showing them how to succeed. I worked intimately with each of them, digging deep, peeling back the layers, all in the name of finding the story of their own life that was holding them back. Each day I worked with incredible people, helping them make breakthroughs in their own lives. And yet here I was, standing in the middle of my own story, a total victim to it.

How the hell was this possible? How had my story held me captive for almost five decades? I could smell a client's story from a mile away, so why couldn't I be the coach to myself? Why couldn't I see or hear my own story?

§ § §

My mom's death was a catalyst for me to spend quality and dedicated time working on my story. I read voraciously, attended workshops, got certified in particular modalities and worked with a psychotherapist in order to try to understand myself better, to gain more insight, and to establish what my story was and how it showed up in my day-to-day life, and how I could manage it moving forward.

When I delved deeper into my life, I began to see that my story started, as most do, when I was a child. Just before my 6th birthday I became a big sister for the second time, and I couldn't wait to see my sibling. She came home tightly swaddled and fast asleep, looking like an angel. She was ceremoniously placed in the middle of my parents' king-size bed. I was ecstatic.

Our home was an explosion of colour and scents: big and small flower arrangements, cakes and biscuits, oh, and my favourite marble cake. Who was all this for? Were the flowers for me, the big sister, congratulating me on the great job I'd done on being a big sister? And all the visitors, who were they coming to see?

Such excitement! There was so much I had to say and tell them about me and my baby sister, and the adventures we were going to have and how I'd been such a star big sister, doing such a good job, which was why Mom and Dad had allowed me to be a big sister again.

I climbed onto the bed to tell my new baby sister about all the people who'd come to visit us, about the marble cake and all the beautiful flowers, and, most importantly, that I was her big sister and that I was so excited to have her home. I wanted to tell her that I would always love her and take care of her as long as she was my baby sister. I was going to be the best, the perfect big sister.

I felt a hard smack on the back of my head. Rough arms picked me up and dumped me on the floor. Then came the angry voice of Mom. 'Don't you do that again! That was naughty. She's small and you can hurt her. Now stay away.'

Now I understand that Mom was tired and that her emotions were running high. She'd just given birth, and she had two other children to think about, and the house being filled with people didn't make it any easier for her. But regardless of how justified Mom's reaction was, that was the start of my story. And, slowly but surely, it grew louder and stronger the older I became.

I'm not good enough.

If I'm not good enough, how can I be loved?

If I'm not good enough, how do I prove to the world that I have worth?

If I'm not good enough, why am I here?

Over time, I learned that to get my mother's approval, I had to be the 'good girl': getting good grades at school, being adult-like and responsible, doing things Mom's way (the right way, the only way), not being a crybaby, not showing 'bad' emotions like anger, knowing my place by being seen and not heard.

Mom was the matriarch. We all marched to her beat, Dad included. Dad, a real softie, never got involved in the arguments between us siblings or intervened in the way that Mom raised or disciplined us.

Every now and then her incredibly high expectations felt exhausting and unsustainable: I'd get less-than-stellar marks in a test and I'd be reprimanded strongly and it felt, in that moment, that Mom had forgotten all the good I'd done in the months prior, that her entire focus was on what I *hadn't* done, on the marks *not* attained.

There were times as a teen that I'd rebel against her, and what I felt were her unfair expectations of me, and I'd not speak to her for months on end. It was always my hope that she'd miss me and invite me back into the fold. Sometimes I'd even instigate a confrontation with her, to see if the make-up process would herald the much desired, 'I love you, let's not do this again.' It never happened.

At 17 I started my first grown-up job, leaving behind my big family – by then I had four siblings – and the sleepy hollow I'd grown up in, and venturing into the 'city of gold' looking for new opportunities, new possibilities and new occasions to re-create me. I worked hard and partied hard – but then the guilt of not being the good girl quickly put me back on the straight and narrow. My upbringing had taught me that good girls work hard but don't party hard – if they partied at all, it was in a decorous manner.

Soon after my move, my parents announced that they, too, were making the trek to Joburg: Dad had a new job and the whole family was relocating. I was ecstatic. I'd get to see my family again and I could show them (well, Mom) how well I was doing – how good I was.

That first Christmas I bought presents for my family with my own hard-earned and hard-saved money. I imagined how proud Mom was going to be, what she was going to say to me. On the day, I climbed out of the car at my parents' house with the bulging bags. 'Look at what I brought for everyone, Mom!' I was practically dancing with excitement – I felt like one of Father Christmas's elves sprinkling fairy dust and magic on everyone.

'That's nice, Juanene,' my mom said, and with a dismissive wave of her hand she turned and headed back to the kitchen.

Then, I felt gutted: all my hard work had been for nothing. Now, I'm able to recognise that in that moment Mom's moving away from me was possibly to ensure that I didn't see her pain: life in the city had turned out to be tougher than she and my dad had expected and the move up to Joburg hadn't born much gold for them.

A few years later I landed a really great job, and I called Mom to share the wonderful news. 'You know you could do better, Juanene,' she said. Now, in hindsight, I recognise that Mom always had incredible dreams for us: she wanted the 'rich and famous' life for us and I suppose her pushing us, egging us on, was her way of ensuring that we made it happen for ourselves. But my interpretation at the time? 'You're not good enough, Juanene.'

I started my own business and called her to tell her about it, bubbling with excitement. 'That's not a real job,' she said. 'You know my sentiments about this hocus-pocus way of yours.' (A 'real job', in Mom's eyes, was a senior corporate role in a stable global organisation.) My interpretation? 'You're not good enough.'

When I hit my first year of seven-figure turnover and invited Mom out for a meal to celebrate, over our risotto and white wine, she said, 'Well, do you know what your brother earns?' My interpretation? 'You're not good enough. Your brother is better.'

When I phoned her with the fabulous news of my first pregnancy, she said, 'I'm not a babysitting service.' My interpretation? 'You're not good enough for me to babysit your children.'

Although at the time, and through those years, these responses of my mom's were devastating to me, now I understand that her own story impacted the way she parented us. She'd had a really hard start to life, and financial security was of paramount importance to her, which led to her constant drive to do more and be more so as to ensure financial stability. She also hadn't been shown much love by her adoptive parents in her formative years, which is why she found it so difficult to show it to others.

In hindsight I recognise that my mom was doing the best she could through the lens of her own story, and that her pushing me was simply her way of ensuring that I was the best version of me that I could possibly be.

§ § §

I realised in the year my mother died that for a long time I'd been living in a mood of resentment. It fuelled me, kept me charged, in motion, always moving towards that elusive state of being good enough and proving it to others. I drove myself hard, wanting to be perfect, to perform, to excel. It played out in my work, my relationships, my studies, my friendships, my career and my parenting.

Along the way, life had offered me many invitations to challenge this story, showing me time and time again that I *was*, in fact, good enough. But I was so hooked into this one way of seeing things that I was unable to see anything else. In fact, often, when I was told I *was* good enough, I didn't believe it.

Some months after my mom's death I attended an enneagram-coaching-related programme. The enneagram is a personality-typing system that describes nine different patterns or ways in which we make sense of the world, as well as showcasing how we manage our thoughts, feelings and actions. Through the insights the enneagram affords, we're able to have a better understanding of ourselves and create alternative ways of being in the world beyond the tired strategies that we've used up to that point.

One lecturer in particular spoke about the 'Strict Perfectionist' personality type, describing it as someone who does the right thing because it's the right thing to do. I recognised myself.

In the days that followed I vacillated between relief at knowing that there were other people like me, and horror at being identified as this particular personality type. But the healing process had begun.

It's been a journey to a space where I'm not held hostage by the undercurrents of my story, and I'm not triggered to revert to old patterns. I now have a set of tools, a map, to enable me to move out of the story into a new set of behaviours. These behaviours support me in becoming a more refined version of myself, allowing me to be more impactful in the work I do, making me a better friend and parent, and, hopefully, one day, a better life partner.

And this is my hope for you: that in these pages, you'll discover your unconscious story and patterns, and that through this discovery, and the suggestions for using these insights, you can create a different, more empowered version of yourself – one in which you and the people around you can delight.

HOW TO USE THIS BOOK

'Damn, I can't believe that I've done [or said] that again!'

Do you find yourself saying this fairly often? If so, I'm confident that by the time you've finished this book, and if you accept and apply the suggestions it offers, you'll be well set to enjoy a life that holds more meaning and harmony.

Being conscious of who we are, what we do and who we're becoming is one of the greatest gifts we can afford ourselves and those around us. The information in the pages that follow will enable you to identify the situations, the people and the events that press your buttons and skyrocket you to a reaction you inevitably regret. You'll understand why you do what you do when someone or something pushes that button, that trigger point that most times you're unaware of or believe that you have under control.

It's not going to be easy. In fact, it may be one of the toughest tasks you'll ever ask of yourself – not many of us relish the thought of hearing about our weaknesses or areas that need development. But reading through the chapters, you may be inspired to try new ways of settling an argument, or to be open to loving your child in a manner unique to them. And in those moments when you realise you haven't been triggered by what someone has said or done, when you grasp that you've chosen a more empowered and elevated way of responding, then you'll know that all your hard work has been worth it.

The animal personality types and their core characteristic

- ✓ Ant: Self-controlled
- ✓ Labrador: Empathetic
- ✓ Eagle: Competitive
- ✓ Black Stallion: Creative
- ✓ Owl: Scholarly
- ✓ Deer: Reliable
- ✓ Butterfly: Versatile
- ✓ Tiger: Courageous
- ✓ Dolphin: Mediator

The unconscious story of each type

- ✓ Ant: 'I'm not good enough.'
- ✓ Labrador: 'I'm unappreciated.'
- ✓ Eagle: 'I can't be insignificant.'
- ✓ Black Stallion: 'I can't be without identity.'
- ✓ Owl: 'I can't be dependent on others or be exhausted.'
- ✓ Deer: 'I'm alone in a threatening world.'
- ✓ Butterfly: 'I can't be limited in any way or be in pain.'
- ✓ Tiger: 'I can't be vulnerable.'
- ✓ Dolphin: 'I can't be controlled or be in turmoil.'

The emotional trigger for each type

An emotional trigger is a deep-seated pressure point that's activated during stressful and emotionally trying times.

- ✓ Ant: Anger
- ✓ Labrador: Pride
- ✓ Eagle: Deceit
- ✓ Black Stallion: Envy
- ✓ Owl: Greed
- ✓ Deer: Fear
- ✓ Butterfly: Gluttony
- ✓ Tiger: Lust
- ✓ Dolphin: Self-forgetting

The shadow of each type

The shadow aspect is that part that remains hidden yet deeply influences our behaviour and plays havoc when unchecked. The shadow side isn't bad; it forms the balance of our two parts, the 'healthy' and 'unhealthy' (or empowered and disempowered) versions of us. For example, there's a difference between having a discerning eye and being judgemental, and between taking charge courageously and being a bulldozing bully.

- ✓ Bee (Ant)
- ✓ Donkey (Labrador)
- ✓ Fox (Eagle)
- ✓ Basset Hound (Black Stallion)
- ✓ Hamster (Owl)
- ✓ Rabbit (Deer)
- ✓ Monkey (Butterfly)
- ✓ Bull (Tiger)
- ✓ Elephant (Dolphin)

Paradoxes and contradictions

As you read, you may find what you would consider to be paradoxical or contradictory information. Bear in mind that we humans have both a healthy and an unhealthy aspect of ourselves, and that there will always be parts of us striving for certain aspects of ourselves that we haven't yet attained. For example, the unconscious story of The Tiger is that they can't be vulnerable (or 'weak'), and for this reason they often show up in the world as strong and sometimes even bullying. But at the same time there's a very different aspect of The Tiger, one that's deeply caring and gentle, and comfortable with her emotions and showing her emotions. And then there's The Tiger that takes considered time to develop a sense of expertise in her professional delivery, and works on containing emotions like rage and anger.

Suggestions for self-growth work

'Self-growth work' refers to areas of ourselves on which we can work. It's the process by which we define our limiting or negative habits and behaviours, and determine practices that support new behaviours, actions and reactions that seek to enable the best versions of ourselves.

Self-check questions

These are questions you can ask yourself to bring your awareness to any given moment, to enable you to pause and bring your attention to your behaviour. If it's your default behaviour, I make suggestions to enable other perspectives and new, healthier behaviours.

Affirmations

An affirmation is a statement made in the first person and present tense, and, most importantly, said in the positive. It isn't enough to just mumble the words; it's how you hold your body when saying the words, and feeling the emotion that the words evoke, that make affirmations the powerful statements they can be.

It's imperative that when saying the affirmation you feel the feeling that the statement evokes in you, for example, if the affirmation is 'I'm acing my interview today', as you say that statement, you need to see in your mind's eye you in the interview room, what you're wearing, how you're sitting, and the feeling of success.

Life lesson

Each animal personality type has an overarching life lesson which, when absorbed and applied, can give us a sense of ease in our lives.

Awareness and paths to greater success

Being aware of our actions, thoughts and behaviours affords us the opportunity of recognising our default patterns and invites us to explore new ways of being and responding to events in our lives.

I provide suggestions for you to work with relative to your emotional, physical and language practices in order to bring a new sense of awareness to each of these aspects of you. Awareness doesn't mean you'll get it right from the start and all the time – you'll never entirely stop the story that runs your life. With these practices, though, you can become aware of your patterns and habitual responses, so that they control you less and less over time.

Reframing your story

'Reframing' is the practice where we see or do something from a different perspective, different to the way we've always seen or done it. The practice of reframing is a coaching technique that allows us to move purposefully and constructively away from a place of confusion or 'stuck-ness'.

The four-breath exercise

This is a physical-awareness exercise that helps to bring your attention to what's going on inside your body and with your emotions by simply following the physical sensation of your breath.

Breathe in slowly for four counts.
Hold your breath for four counts.
Breathe out slowly for four counts.
Repeat this for four rounds, slowing it more each time.
Focus on taking slow, full breaths, down into your belly.

If you start feeling overwhelmed, bring your attention back to your breath and notice things in your physical environment. Listen for sounds, feel the air temperature and your feet on the floor.

Change your words, change your story

Over the years I've seen, very practically, that the language we speak and the thoughts we have impact our biology – the stories we tell about ourselves have an impact on who we are and who we become.

For example, imagine you're talking about a recent holiday, and you describe it using words like 'fantastic', 'best', 'luxurious' … you get the picture. As you're telling this story, your body – the biology of you – reacts, feeling the emotions that mirror these words, and you feel momentarily carefree and happy.

Now imagine recounting a story of a disagreement you recently had with a colleague, using words such as 'confrontational', 'inflexible' and 'volatile'. Again, without having to do anything other than recount the story, your body will be triggered by your vocabulary and will become tense and stressed and angry or sad.

In this way, our biography becomes our biology: our inner narrative impacts our external personality and our personal reality.

What is the enneagram?

The enneagram (from the Greek *ennéa* meaning 'nine', and *grámma* meaning something written or drawn) is a typing system of nine interconnected personality types that makes visible for us how we interpret our engagement in the world, and how we can use this insight to support our journey of self-development. The history and origins of the enneagram are unclear but it seems to be reflected in different spiritual and religious traditions from earliest times.

The traditional enneagram personality types are:

The animal personalities in this book are my take on the traditional enneagram, with its wisdom, its teachings that enable us to be the fullest versions of ourselves, and, most importantly, the lessons we learn when we understand the 'why' of what we do.

FIND YOUR ANIMAL PERSONALITY TYPE

There isn't a right or wrong way of learning about yourself, or a time frame – other than your entire life. My suggestion is that you simply be curious as to what animal type you are and how this plays out in the various aspects of your life.

We all have all nine types in us although usually one is by far the most prominent. It has been, and will continue to be, your key story until the end of time. The others are rather like the supporting acts to your main show.

When reading through the descriptors, it's vital that you pay attention to the *inner story* of each animal personality type, because that's what determines whether you're that type or not. You're not a particular animal personality type because you recognise the behaviours in yourself. For example, many of us can act like a bully (The Tiger) or have a lurking perfectionist within (The Ant), but that doesn't mean we all resonate with the core story of either ('I can't be vulnerable' and 'I can't be not good enough'). You're a type because of the core story of that type.

One or two of the animal types may set you thinking to yourself, *Hmm … that's kinda me*. There might be those that you think have a smidgen of you. And then you may find that one of the animal types makes you feel exceptionally uncomfortable, a little hot under the collar – and that could be because that type is, in fact, you.

Once you've established which animal type you are, dip into the types on either side. The types on either side of our core type are somewhat like the training wheels on a bicycle in that they can act like stabilisers. In my own case as The Ant, for example, when I operate in the world from my 'healthy' state, I can scoop up the healthy aspects of both The Labrador and The Dolphin: I can be gentle and loving towards myself when I mess up and am not perfect, and equally I can be kind towards others when they don't get stuff right (by my terms); and I can listen with understanding to other perspectives without judging them as right or wrong, and I can take decisions that are right for me in spite of perhaps creating turmoil for others.

There will be times, of course, when I'm in my 'unhealthy' (shadow) state, and The Bee is stinging everyone in sight, and I become the martyr and believe that no-one loves me (The Donkey), and passive-aggressive in my behaviour (The Elephant).

'Using the lines'

In the enneagram, each personality type is connected by lines to two other types. You can gain another layer of insight and learning by scooping from the healthy attributes of the type at the end of the line. For example as The Ant, in my healthy state I also have the ability to access the healthy states of The Butterfly (spontaneity) and The Black Stallion (creativity); and in my unhealthy state I tap into the unhealthy states of these types – scatteredness and drama.

✓ The Tiger: practise healthy aspects of The Labrador and The Owl.
✓ The Dolphin: practise healthy aspects of The Eagle and The Deer.
✓ The Ant: practise healthy aspects of The Butterfly and The Black Stallion.
✓ The Labrador: practise healthy aspects of The Tiger and The Black Stallion.
✓ The Eagle: practise healthy aspects of The Deer and The Dolphin.
✓ The Black Stallion: practise healthy aspects of The Labrador and The Ant.
✓ The Owl: practise healthy aspects of The Butterfly and The Tiger.
✓ The Deer: practise healthy aspects of The Dolphin and The Eagle.
✓ The Butterfly: practise healthy aspects of The Ant and The Owl.

Quick pick: which of these statements most applies to you?

❑ 'I have to do the right thing': you're probably The Ant
❑ 'I have to be liked and appreciated': you're probably The Labrador
❑ 'I have to outshine the rest': you're probably The Eagle
❑ 'I have to be unique': you're probably The Black Stallion
❑ 'I have to understand': you're probably The Owl
❑ 'I have to be safe and belong': you're probably The Deer
❑ 'I have to experience it all': you're probably The Butterfly
❑ 'I have to be strong and in control': you're probably The Tiger
❑ 'I have to keep the balance': you're probably The Dolphin

THE ANT

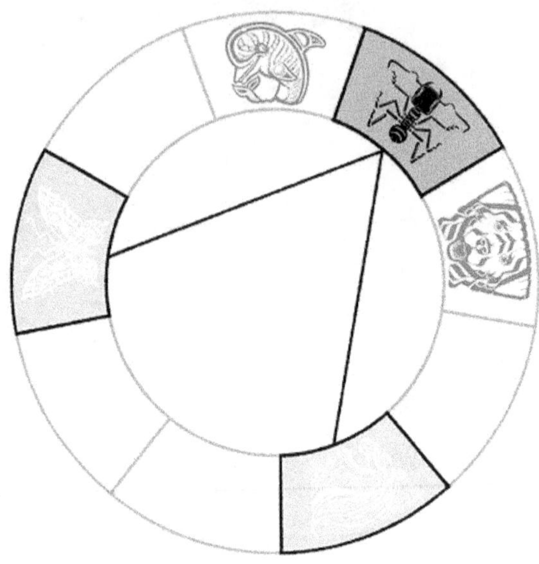

Also known as The Reformer, The Strict Perfectionist or The Good Person.

The Ant is driven by personal integrity and self-control. Ants are known for their honesty, dependability and common sense. They have a deep need to improve themselves, others and the world. They have a definite sense of right and wrong, and hold themselves and others to incredibly high ethical standards and behaviours.

Inner story:	'I'm not good enough.'
Core motivation:	'I have to do the right and good thing.'
Emotional trigger:	Anger – although Ants don't necessarily show it outright as they consider it a 'bad' emotion. An Ant's anger may leak out in the form of sarcasm, irritation, resentment, a disapproving frown or a tightening of the jaw.
Superpower:	Integrity.
Key characteristics:	<ul><li>Self-controlled</li><li>Self-disciplined</li><li>Very conscientious</li><li>Exceptionally ethical</li><li>Analytical</li></ul>
Challenges:	<ul><li>Rigid in body, emotion and language</li><li>Controlling</li><li>Judgemental</li><li>Overly critical</li><li>Aloof</li></ul>
Striving for:	Serenity; a letting-go of how things and people, including themselves, should be.
Value:	Goodness. Ants have a need to make the world a better place.
Speaking style:	Precise, clear, direct, honest and detail-oriented, prone to sermonising.
Don't like:	Relaxing, time wasting, spontaneity.

THE LABRADOR

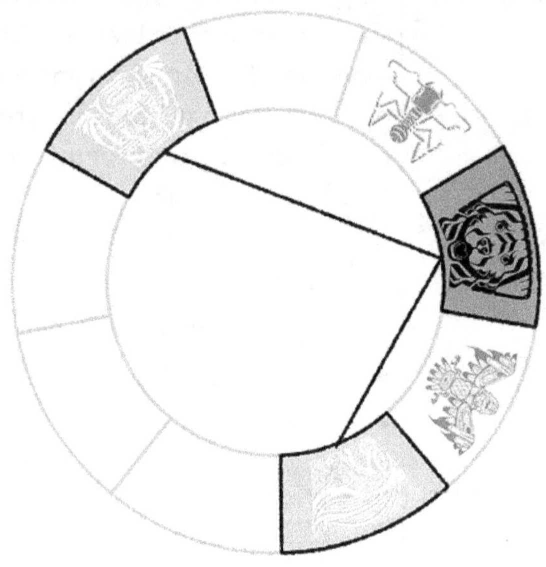

Also known as The Helper, The Giver or The Lover.

Labradors are deeply caring, empathic, warm and considerate. They have a generally helpful view on life and the way they act in the world, giving service. Labradors are often so focused on supporting others that they forget their own needs and are devastated when their love and attention aren't reciprocated.

Inner story:	'I'm unloved, unappreciated.'
Core motivation:	'I have to be liked and appreciated.'
Emotional trigger:	Pride – in how indispensable they are to the people around them and how things fall apart when they aren't present.
Superpower:	Caring.
Key characteristics:	• Empathetic • Appreciative • Generous • Socially responsive • Cheerful
Challenges:	• Dependent on approval of others • Privileged • Seductive • Insincere • Martyr
Striving for:	Humility; the ability to ask for and accept help, love and acknowledgement for themselves.
Value:	Love. Labradors value and are attracted to love and wish to foster loving relationships with themselves and all around them, thereby making the world a more loving place.
Speaking style:	Kind and sympathetic, tend to give unsolicited advice.
Don't like:	Putting self first, bullying, rejection.

THE EAGLE

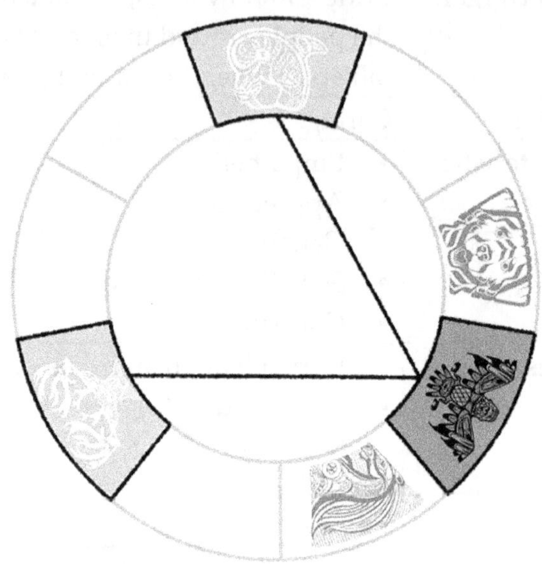

Also known as *The Performer, The Chameleon* or *The Competitive Achiever.*

Eagles are task-oriented, assertive, efficient and industrious: everyone wants The Eagle on their team. The worldview of The Eagle is that only winners are recognised. Eagles are goal-oriented: they know exactly what they want from life and they move directly towards that target. They're tireless in achieving their desired outcomes, and are incredibly agile and adept at creating new iterations of themselves so as to align with their desires.

Inner story:	'I can't be insignificant or useless.'
Core motivation:	'I have to outshine the rest.'
Emotional trigger:	Deceit – often of themselves, as Eagles are known to project an air of being the best even when they know they're not.
Superpower:	Persistence.
Key characteristics:	• Self-assured • Ambitious • Competitive • Energetic • Charming
Challenges:	• Image-driven • Over-worked • Impatient • Unhealthily competitive • Self-promoting
Striving for:	Veracity; the knowing that they have immense value for who they are as they are and not what they do.
Value:	Productivity and efficiency.
Speaking style:	Enthusiastic, topic-focused, fast-paced and confident, impatient, overly efficient, overriding of others' views.
Don't like:	Being still for the sake of being still, failure, spending time on exploring emotions, not winning.

THE BLACK STALLION

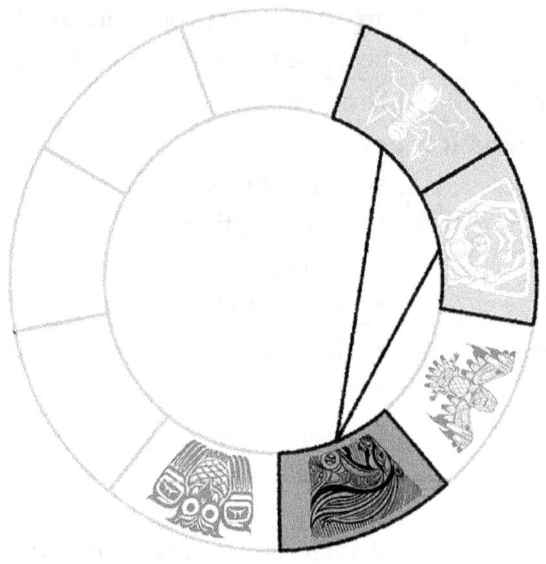

Also known as The Individualist, The Tragic Romantic or The Intense Creative.

Black Stallions are intuitive, sensitive to emotions and feelings (theirs and others'), romantic and imaginative. At their best they're creative, inspired, self-aware and emotionally strong. They're intensely creative in both their inner and outer worlds. Black Stallions have a deep desire to be authentic and are known for their individuality. They don't want to be 'beige', the same as everyone else.

Inner story:	'I can't be without identity.'
Core motivation:	'I have to be unique.'
Emotional trigger:	Envy – Black Stallions believe on some level that there's something missing from their life, and they may envy someone else for something they own or a relationship they have, or just for who they are.
Superpower:	Aesthete.
Key characteristics:	• Creative • Empathetic • Idealistic • Capable of emotional depth • Compassion
Challenges:	• Moody • Withdrawn • Self-absorbed • Oversensitive • Demanding • Unsatisfied by what is
Striving for:	Equanimity; a state of stillness beyond their swirling emotions.
Value:	Originality. Black Stallions value being themselves.
Speaking style:	Expressive of feelings, personal, self-focused, have a flair for originality, may be perceived as overly expressive, unsatisfied by responses and emotionally intense.
Don't like:	Ordinariness, being alone for too long, being devoid of emotion.

THE OWL

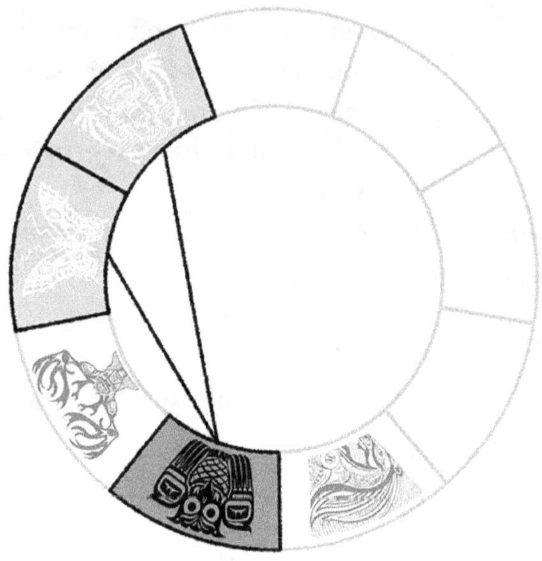

Also known as The Thinker, The Quiet Specialist or The Investigator.

Owls are perceptive, secretive, focused, curious and detached. They wish to understand the world – knowledge excites them. They'd far rather be alone with their thoughts than spend time with people, unless they find a kindred spirit whose intellect and knowledge they admire.

Inner story:	'I can't be exhausted. I can't be dependent on others.'
Core motivation:	'I have to understand.'
Emotional trigger:	Greed – for information and knowledge; but miserly with sharing it.
Superpower:	Investigator.
Key characteristics:	<ul><li>Scholarly</li><li>Perceptive</li><li>Objective</li><li>Insightful</li><li>Independent</li></ul>
Challenges:	<ul><li>Detached</li><li>Isolated</li><li>Stingy with knowledge</li><li>Unsociable</li><li>Indifferent</li></ul>
Striving for:	Non-attachment; letting go of the need to hoard resources such as time and energy, and trust that it will all be present, in abundance, when required.
Value:	Wisdom. Owls value a deep understanding of a matter or subject.
Speaking style:	Content-focused, clear, analytical and wordy, not big on small talk, may be perceived as emotionally disconnected, aloof, overanalytical and distant, rational and technical, most comfortable in their area of expertise.
Don't like:	Being with emotions, intrusions into their lives, a 'light' version of life.

THE DEER

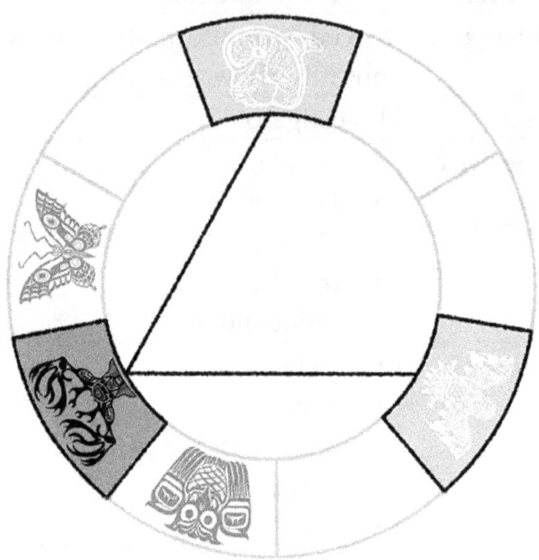

Also known as Devil's Advocate, The Troubleshooter or The Loyal Skeptic.

The Deer is reliable, security-oriented and vigilant, courageous, funny, affectionate and warm. Deers are brain-driven, using their vigilance to anticipate problems, find solutions and establish rules and procedures that create a sense of security. It's important for Deers to ensure a stable environment for themselves while managing their inner anxieties.

Inner story:	'I'm alone in a threatening world.'
Core motivation:	'I have to be safe and belong.'
Emotional trigger:	Fear itself.
Superpower:	Discernment.
Key characteristics:	• Loyal • Reliable • Hardworking • Responsible
Challenges:	• Anxious • Hyper-vigilant • Pessimistic • Suspicious • Doubtful
Striving for:	Courage; the Deer needs to know that they have what's needed to be safe in the world.
Value:	Loyalty.
Speaking style:	Thoughtful, contrary, questioning, information-oriented; may be seen as pessimistic, challenging, doubting or controlling.
Don't like:	Lack of information, irresponsibility, a state of unpreparedness.

THE BUTTERFLY

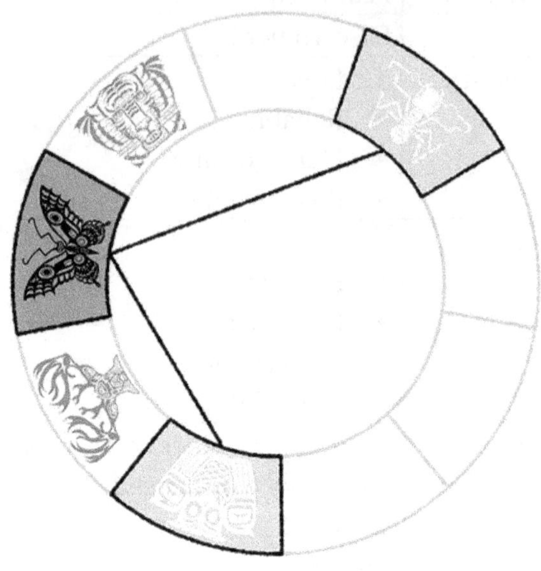

Also known as The Dreamer, The Enthusiastic Visionary or The Dilettante.

The Butterfly is enthusiastic, fast-talking, spontaneous, versatile and excitable. Of all the personality types, The Butterfly is the best at handling the large amounts of information and stimuli that characterise our modern society — a perfect example of the 'monkey-mind' that's constantly distracted by thoughts and finds it difficult to be in the present moment. Butterflies are visionary, modern and exciting. They have a contagious energy, yet don't seem to be able to enjoy what they have in the present and tend to wish for what they don't have — that which appears elusive.

Inner story:	'I can't be limited. I can't be in pain.'
Core motivation:	'I have to experience it all.'
Emotional trigger:	Gluttony – for whatever life can offer.
Superpower:	Newness.
Key characteristics:	• Adventurous • Fun-loving • Quick-thinking • Versatile • Playful
Challenges:	• Dispersed • Uncommitted • Scattered • Undisciplined • Over-extended
Striving for:	Sobriety; a sense of focusing on what they have and not what's missing, and knowing that what they have is enough.
Value:	Joy.
Speaking style:	Either very entertaining or self-absorbed; focus on the positive, tend to ignore the negative; exuberant, fast-paced, spontaneous; may be perceived as quickly shifting topics, making excuses, indifferent to others' input.
Don't like:	The mundane, repetition, being in the now, experiencing pain.

THE TIGER

Also known as The Active Controller, The Challenger or The Protector.

The Tiger is independent, action-oriented, straight-talking and assertive. Tigers have a great instinctual energy and are natural leaders. They fight for justice in a world they see as unfair. For The Tiger, it's easy to get angry but difficult to express vulnerable feelings. Tigers present a tough exterior to the world while underneath that apparently impenetrable pelt lies a deep sense of vulnerability.

Inner story:	'I can't be vulnerable.'
Core motivation:	'I have to be in control.'
Emotional trigger:	Lust – tendency towards excess, emotionally, mentally or physically.
Superpower:	Confidence.
Key characteristics:	• Courageous • Strong • Determined • Generous • Protective of others
Challenges:	• Excessive • Domineering • Confrontational • Vengeful • Defiant
Striving for:	Innocence; being vulnerable, open hearted and without cynicism.
Value:	Strength. Tigers like to use their power to ensure that the world is more just.
Speaking style:	Direct, authoritative, firm and oriented to truth and justice; may be perceived as confrontational, intimidating, loud and controlling.
Don't like:	Demonstrating soft emotions and vulnerability, injustice, lack of control.

THE DOLPHIN

Also known as The Mediator, The Adaptive Peacemaker or The Facilitator.

Dolphins are the diplomatic facilitators and mediators of the world. They often say 'yes' when they mean 'no', just to keep the peace. On the surface they appear to be happy to go with the flow but underneath they're suppressing a deep, unconscious store of anger. This concealed wrath comes from the story Dolphins tell themselves: that it's more important to keep the peace than speak up for themselves.

Inner story:	'I can't be controlled. I can't be in turmoil.'
Core motivation:	'I have to keep the peace. I have to create a sense of harmony.'
Emotional trigger:	Self-forgetting. Dolphins disengage from and forget their own needs and instead focus on those of others.
Superpower:	Perspective.
Key characteristics:	• Excellent mediators • Harmonious • Inclusive • Diplomatic • Engaged
Challenges:	• Passive-aggressive • Easily distracted • Stubborn • Resigned
Striving for:	Remembering of self. Acting on priorities that are important and of value to them.
Value:	Harmony and peace.
Speaking style:	Non-confrontational, friendly, focusing on others; scattered, unclear and overly conciliatory; may have trouble getting to the point.
Don't like:	Negative or disturbing people or instances, making hasty decisions, conflict, drastic change.

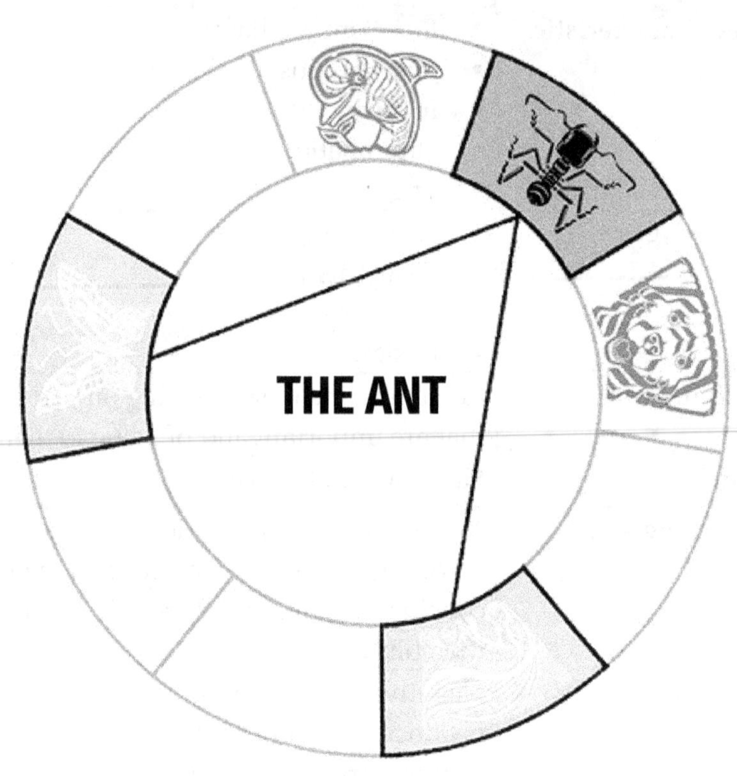
THE ANT

'An ant can hurt an elephant'
– African proverb

Well-known Ants

Nelson Mandela, Mahatma Gandhi, Michelle Obama, Hillary Clinton, Celine Dion, Martha Stewart, Jane Fonda, Meryl Streep, Harrison Ford.

Other names for the Ant

The Reformer, The Strict Perfectionist or The Good Person.

Are you an Ant? Do you:

- Often say things like 'I must…', 'I have to…', I need to…'?
- Live with a strong strict inner critic that monitors your thoughts, words and deeds?
- Feel 100% responsible for making things right?
- Get angry when others don't do the right thing, or when important rules and standards are ignored?
- Feel disillusioned and deeply disappointed when things go wrong?
- See yourself as a giver and, often, others as takers?
- Feel you're often overinvolved and that others are underinvolved?
- Sometimes lash out or be sarcastic and cutting?
- Look for love and approval from others by being good and right?
- Have a cause (or many) you're involved in?
- Pride yourself on your quick mind and intellectual prowess?

The Ant is represented as type 1 in the enneagram.

Ants are often called Reformers because they have a 'sense of mission' that leads them to want to reform the world. They believe that if they ran the world, it would be a good place to live in and things would get done in the right way. Ants will take on more work than necessary and will often burden themselves redoing work because of a minor error instead of handing it back and asking for the rework to be done by the originator. If they've delegated work and don't believe that it's being done well enough, they'll take the work back and do it themselves, all in the pursuit of 'good enough' and perfection.

Ants are driven by personal integrity and self-control. They're known for their honesty, dependability and common sense. They're also most concerned that others, and the world, do the right thing.

Some people call Ants 'Strict Perfectionists' – and they are! They have exceptionally high standards for both themselves and others, and are on a mission to perfect themselves, others and the world at large. This mission may lead Ants to feel an element of self-sacrifice and, as a result, resentment towards others.

Triggers for The Ant

- Feeling or being deceived.
- Lack of integrity from others.
- Being criticised.
- When others don't show up or don't follow through: 'If you say you're going to do something by 10am on Wednesday morning, 10am is 9.50am and not 10.15am!'
- A change in plans they didn't agree to: 'If you're going to change a plan that concerns me, ask me, don't just make a unilateral decision where I'm concerned.'
- Mistakes or things not being perfect, regardless of the size or importance: typographical errors and imperfections in a job will trigger The Ant every bit as much as someone wearing black stockings with beige shoes.

The Ant's unconscious story: 'I'm not good enough'

The core story for the Ant is the deeply held idea of 'I'm not good, perfect or right enough'. And as crazy as it sounds, the state of enough-ness is never attained. The inner critic hammers hard every day, incessantly chattering, criticising and egging on The Ant to be better, closer to perfect or more right.

Ants operate under a constant state of self-flagellation and criticism. 'I have to work hard [or harder]' is a well-known mantra.

Ants mostly work *harder* rather than *smarter*, even when they can see the smarter option. Workaholics, they're constantly looking for what's wrong in their lives (and in the world) and, as far as they're concerned, there's always room for improvement.

They have a black-and-white way of engaging with the world: they're going to do life either the right way or not at all.

If you're constantly looking for what's wrong, you'll find it. The Ant always does. They see themselves as being in a state of imperfection and a work in progress.

For Ants, anger is a 'not good' emotion and, as much as they believe they manage their anger, they generally don't express it in a healthy way. They tend to carry their anger in the rigidity of their bodies, biting down on it instead of voicing it: this can be seen in a tightening of their jaw and even grinding their teeth. Ants may have a 'carrot up the butt' stance and squareness in their shoulders, as they often carry tension here.

The healthy Ant

Healthy versions of The Ant show up in the world as creative, inventive and spontaneous. They're also more accepting of faults – those of others and of their own making. They're wise and discerning, and take the time to consider different ways of being and acting. They're able to consider the perspectives of others and feel comfortable accepting criticism and feedback.

When the Ant can accept that not everything has to be perfect – that nothing can be better than that particular outcome – their mood will lighten almost immediately. If they can laugh at themselves and recognise that it can't be 'my way is the only way', they're able to relax more and be more open to what else is possible.

It's tough for The Ant to see shades of grey. They tend to see in polarities of black and white, right and wrong. But if they can see the spaces and the nuances of the concept of grey, they feel calmer and more serene; they have the ability to be principled and ethical yet not dictatorial and rigid.

Healthy Ants have also mastered the challenge of having fun. They think nothing of heading out to a movie midweek or dancing with abandon even though to the world it may look as though they have two left feet. Spontaneity might initially be a considered act, but in time they're able to be less tied into their sense of responsibility, and with mindful work they find a way to live and love life to the full, in the most carefree and childlike manner.

The unhealthy Ant: The Bee

The Bee, like The Ant, is industrious, but the difference between the two is that The Bee has a sting. When The Ant's 'Strict Perfectionist' self feels as though something isn't in order or isn't being done to their levels of perfection, The Bee stings by sending out a scathing email, or lashing out and belittling someone. Many Bees would call this their 'dark sense of humour' or their 'quick wit' and would see nothing wrong in their behaviour, perhaps even commending themselves on their verbal prowess. Bees can also smile through the anger and resentment – an attempt to appear polite, because being polite is what 'good' people do.

Bees often suffer getting caught up in trying to get everything perfectly done before putting it out into the world, which leads to unnecessary delays: because their internal narrative tells them to do things perfectly, procrastination results in an inability to actually get stuff done.

The Ant at work

Ants have a certain standard on which they're not prepared to compromise. They may say (or think), 'Unless I can find a person of the right standard, I'd rather not subcontract because it affects my reputation and the quality of the product I deliver.'

Whether a colleague or boss, The Ant is hard to please at work. Ants are highly ethical and virtuous, and keenly focused on doing the right thing. This means that you, as their colleague, need to do the right thing. If you don't, The Ant will judge you.

At their worst, Ants can be vocally sharp and cutting when triggered. It might sound like, 'How many times do you need to do this before you get it right?'

Because The Ant's internal story is that they can do everything better than everyone else and that theirs is the right and only approach, the art of delegation is definitely an area of development for this animal personality type.

Ant leaders can be rigid, controlling and dictatorial (and not benign dictators, either). They expect everyone to march with the same military precision. They're also known to micro-manage and over-control their subordinates because they believe they know best.

Ants can make impulsive decisions if they believe they're being criticised or their ethics are being questioned, and then they regret these decisions.

The Ant in relationships

Ants are faithful. They seek out their own development, whether as a parent or a life partner, sincerely wanting to be the healthiest version of themselves. They're able to let go of the need to be responsible for everything and everyone. On the other hand, they can be resentful and uncompromising.

As a parent they can be critical and unwavering in their rules and regulations. As healthy versions of themselves, they can support their children by setting boundaries and enabling age-appropriate accountability and responsibility.

AN ANT'S STORY: BANISHING CRUELLA

Lucy was a 30-something chemical engineer working in a predominantly male environment. She had graduated top of her class at school and was a cum laude graduate at university. Now she had her PhD in her sights but the closer she got to the end of her paper and to her submission date, the louder the negative self-talk became.

She spoke of second-guessing herself and her paper, of how she would spend hours reading other PhDs' work and berate herself for her paper not being up to theirs. She mentioned how her internal criticism and belittling were getting so out of hand, the internal noise of her not being good enough so constant, that there were days that she simply sat and stared at her laptop, not adding a single paragraph to her thesis.

We co-designed a few approaches to manage the critic: we gave her a name – Cruella – and Lucy worked on being aware of what brought Cruella rushing to the front of her mind, such as comparisons with others. We also worked on how Lucy could balance, with evidence, examples of where she had 'done good' when Cruella raised her criticism.

I suggested that Lucy stop reading other papers; that she create some space for lighthearted fun; that she write in spaces that created a sense of calm, such as at the bottom of her garden; and that, at the end of each day, she wrote down, for herself, three things that she'd done that she was proud of.

What she'd hoped would be a four-year PhD process ended up being just shy of five years, but along the way Lucy was able to repair the relationship between herself and her internal critic. She was able to be kinder and more accepting of herself, and not set herself up for possible failure with the unattainable goals of the past.

Self-growth work

Possible areas of focus:

- Seeing the spectrum of grey in life (not just black and white).
- Being less judgemental of self and others.
- Loosening up a little.
- Getting life wrong from time to time.
- Colouring outside the lines in life.

Focus more on people than on tasks

Ants are far nicer to be around when they connect from the heart and not about the task at hand. In these moments they're approachable and collaborative, and less judgemental. Nobody (not even The Ant) is a machine. Ants can work on recognising that mistakes will happen, that people may let them down and that cutting some slack will go a long way in forging relationships.

Self-check questions
How might I work smarter rather than harder?
What part of this relationship brings me joy?

Affirmations
I am good enough.
This isn't important in the bigger picture, so I'm letting it go.

Being fluid in the way they work

Ants are regimented by design and behaviour, so it's of incredible benefit to them to explore different marches and tunes, and to understand that there are many different routes and approaches to attaining the same result. The challenge is to recognise black-

or-white thinking, and to move out of that state of what has to be perfect and what isn't perfect, to allow shades of grey.

Self-check questions
If I had to choose the most important things to focus on today/this week/
this month, what are they?
What can I let go of to support the bigger picture?

Affirmations
I'm flexible in my way of being, and manage change with grace.
I'm curious as to what else is possible.

Just chill

Make time to relax. Schedule a daily practice (even if it's only 10 minutes) for *dolce far niente* – pleasantly doing nothing. It may be simply to bask in the sun without reading the latest *Harvard Business Review*. Have a decadent midweek siesta or sip a glass of champagne before lunch. Because The Ant would consider this to be lazy and unproductive, it will take conscious work and practice.

Self-check questions
How might making time for doing nothing benefit me and
those around me?
What form could dolce far niente (the sweetness of doing nothing)
take for me?

Affirmations
I connect with what is peaceful around me.
I make time for me each day.

Look up

Look up and see the bigger picture. If The Ant could rise above the task, as The Butterfly might, they would see what else is happening and enjoy a broader perspective. They would then be able to be the observer of themselves. When we create a space of distance between ourselves and our story, we're afforded the opportunity of observing ourselves and our behaviours without being caught up in the drama of the behaviour.

Self-check questions
What other possibilities may exist?
What might the bigger picture look like in this instance?

Affirmations
I'm taking a step back so that I can see the bigger picture.
I'm able to observe my behaviours without being caught up in the drama.

Let it go

Ants can very easily get into a lather about others' shortcomings. They love to point out inaccuracies. Ants don't necessarily consciously look for mistakes; it's as if mistakes find them. In a restaurant, Ants will notice spelling errors on the menu, and if they're unable to let it go, it's possible their entire experience will be ruined. Unconsciously, they'll start looking for what else is wrong: the service is slow, or their fries aren't crispy. Ants need to notice and minimise their impatience with themselves and others, and learn the art of letting things go.

Play more

There's truth in the adage 'all work and no play make Jack a dull boy'. Part of The Ant's journey towards change is to be lighter and have more fun. Jump on a bicycle, go dancing, say yes to invitations, go to a comedy show, play a board game. A good beginning would be to do something creative: paint, bake, write a poem.

When we're able to be playful in ourselves, it's so much easier for the people in our lives to be lighter too. There's no need to have 'perfect' fun when you're simply having fun.

AN ANT'S STORY: THE ART OF DELEGATION

Everything in Sheila's life appeared perfectly staged, even her salads. In her deeply rooted story of everything having to be perfect and that she alone could make things that way, she realised that she'd missed out on many occasions to allow creativity to simply flow.

In our sessions, Sheila and I worked together exploring what her fears may have been in letting go of certain tasks or delegating aspects of a project. It was soon evident that the hidden voice told her that if any aspect of the project or task wasn't perfectly executed – and by 'perfectly' she meant her levels of extraordinary perfection – that she alone would be singled out as not good enough.

We spoke about creativity and how she might figuratively colour outside the lines. We looked at how, even though her inner critic might tell her that her piece of art wasn't good enough and that she should stop immediately lest anyone find out, she should continue exploring her unique way of expressing this aspect of herself.

'I've learned to relax a lot on things, including non-work-related matters. For example, I still prefer to have my salads done in a particular way and the food I put out presented in a specific way. And I still take great pride in doing them in a specific creative way and I admire the end product and feel super proud.

'But this isn't related to my purpose in the world. Now, when I don't have the time to do something, as happened recently at my birthday party, I'll ask another person to do it. It ended up looking very different from how I would've done it. I looked at it and thought, *Mmm, not the way I would've done it at all, but it's not bad and it's certainly a different way of looking at it ...* It was a hard concession for me, but I'm working on it.'

Paths to greater success

Life lesson

To change what can be changed, to accept what can't be changed, and to develop the wisdom to know the difference.

Emotional awareness practice

Step 1: Name the emotion

What are you feeling? Name the emotion.

Ants get angry easily but battle to notice or admit it. They may say, 'I'm pissed off. This isn't right. I'm frustrated.' But they never say, 'I'm angry.'

Anger can be a healthy emotion. Accessed constructively, it brings powerful positive change.

Step 2: Find the story

What's the story you're telling about yourself, the situation or the other person?

- *I've been criticised.*
- *I should've known better.*
- *I feel blindsided.*
- *I was right and they were wrong.*

Step 3: Reframe the story

If there was a neutral observer to this situation, what story might they tell? What might a different story be that you're not seeing?

- *Is there another way this could play out?*
- *Is it possible my team member didn't have all the information at hand at the time?*
- *Am I jumping to conclusions?*

- *How might I experience life as abundant rather than lacking?*

Physical awareness practice

In Ants we see a pattern of top-down control. They tend to hold their tension and control around the jaw, neck and shoulders. They also tend to tense and constrict their diaphragm and take shallow breaths.

As soon as you notice yourself doing this, move. Stand up. Walk around. Close the laptop. Walk out of the room. Take a bathroom break. Stretch. In your triggered state you may want to lash out verbally. The aim of moving is to enable you to gain perspective.

Do the breathing exercise recommended on page 29.

Practise physical relaxation and allow the pleasure of life to grow without trying to control everything.

Language awareness practice

The words of The Ant are often:

- ✗ *I must.*
- ✗ *I have to.*
- ✗ *I need to.*
- ✗ *I ought to.*
- ✗ *I should.*
- ✗ *It's right.*
- ✗ *It's wrong.*

Instead try one of the following more empowered options:

- ✓ *I choose to.*
- ✓ *It could be fun to try that.*
- ✓ *Why not?*
- ✓ *It's possible.*
- ✓ *I can laugh at that.*

AN ANT'S STORY: STUCK AND CAN'T PROGRESS

Tom was a senior financial manager. At age 48, he felt he just wasn't progressing. 'I was stuck. My professional and personal relationships weren't ideal. But I wasn't sure why, or what, I was doing wrong.'

When he read the key characteristics of The Ant, he immediately recognised his need to be good or right. 'At work this often meant I simply did things myself so I could be sure they'd be done correctly. Becoming aware of these key characteristics was a game-changer for me as a leader. I started to see that by doing the work myself I didn't empower the people around me.'

Tom was surprised to recognise that, at the core of his person, he was self-doubting, with little self-confidence. 'That often meant I didn't make decisions and I tended to go with whatever anyone else decided. This indecision and procrastination stemmed from me wanting to do the right thing, say the right thing, all the time, and because I was generally not sure if it was or wasn't, I didn't take action. I now hold myself accountable in meetings to speak up, even if it means that what I want to say isn't perfectly constructed, or if my audience doesn't fully grasp what I'm saying and I have to clarify my comment or suggestion.

'My defence – or attack – mode was to lash out sarcastically when I didn't get my way rather than discussing the situation constructively. At home this was more prevalent, and my wife complained I was sarcastic and domineering.

'Although my daughter has an average of 80% at school, I've always felt she could do better and told her that the whole time. I'm working now on congratulating her more.

'Nowadays I pause and take a breath before voicing my opinion, ensuring that I'm not reacting in the old behaviour of lashing out and being sarcastic.

'I've learned that although it has always been my belief that my work demands that I'm 100% correct at all times, this isn't so because that wouldn't be possible for a mere mortal. This insight has allowed me to relax in my personal life as well.

'These days I'm aware of my emotions and I'm able to name them, especially my anger and resentment, whereas before I wasn't aware of them at all. I'm learning to think before I speak as opposed to apologising afterwards.

THE LABRADOR

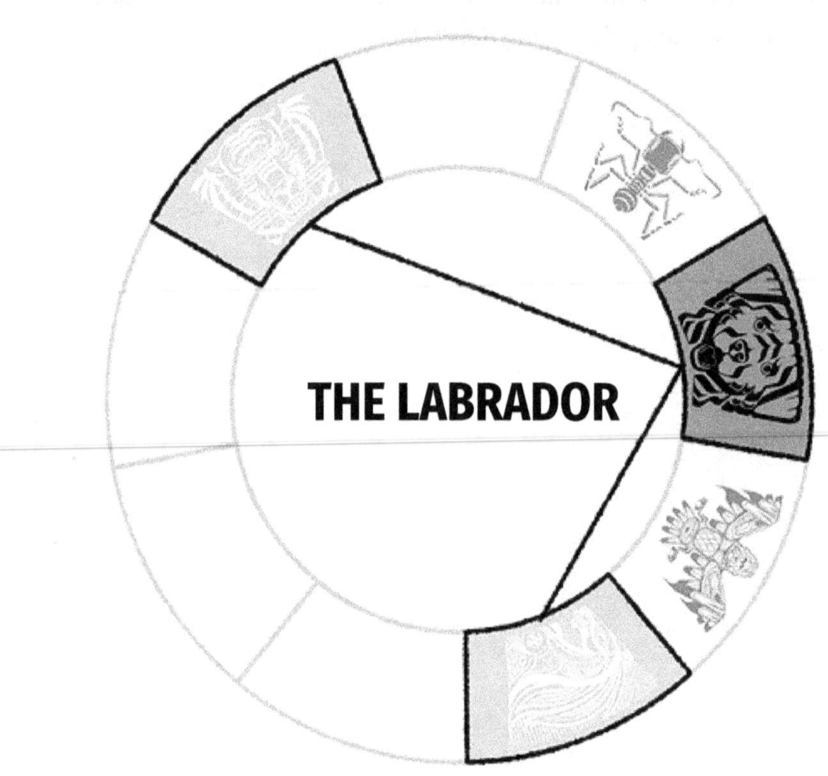

'Dogs don't actually prefer bones to meat; it is just that no one ever gives them meat.'
- *African proverb*

Well-known Labradors

Desmond Tutu, Dolly Parton, Lionel Richie, Stevie Wonder, Monica Lewinsky, Luciano Pavarotti, Byron Katie.

Other names for the Labrador

The Helper, The Giver or The Lover.

Are you a Labrador? Do you:
- Focus on the needs of others?
- Take pride in giving and helping?
- Sometimes feel that people take advantage of you?
- Find it difficult to express your own needs?
- Avoid asking for help and don't easily accept it when it's given?
- Not have strong boundaries?
- Sometimes come across as martyr-like because of all the giving you dole out and the belief that you don't receive in return?

The Labrador is represented as type 2 in the enneagram.

The dog is man's best friend, and you can't ask for a better friend than a Labrador. They're deeply caring, empathic, warm and considerate. However bad your day has been, a Labrador brightens it with the welcome you get at the front door, sloppy kisses and all.

Labrador personality types have a keen sense of alertness to potential danger to their loved ones, and will protect them whenever necessary. They show immense loyalty and devotion to those they love.

This behaviour is core: Labradors will neglect themselves completely while supporting others, including putting aside their own dreams and desires to help others achieve theirs. True considerate helpers, Labradors position themselves, and their lives, as acts of service to others.

The inner desire of The Labrador is to be appreciated, acknowledged and loved, and sometimes, in order to attain this, they become emotionally manipulative: they love in order to be loved in return. It's not something to which they would consciously own up or even recognise. The aspect of manipulation is hidden for Labradors, who're mostly unaware of their motivation of giving to get.

Triggers for The Labrador

- Feeling that they're being taken for granted.
- A culture or mood of disrespect for people.
- Lack of consideration of other people's feelings.
- Exclusion from meetings or events that previously involved them or that others know interest them.
- Feeling unappreciated or valueless.
- Accusations of being manipulative.

The Labrador's unconscious story: 'I can't be unloved'

The underlying story of the Labrador is one that constantly feeds their greatest fear, that of being unloved. The thought process of The Labrador plays out something like this: *If I do all the loving and giving, at some point someone will recognise that I'm worthy of being loved back.* They will, for example, give you their jersey because you're cold, and never mind that they're freezing.

Labradors have a hard time saying no. In their desire to care for others, they'll put themselves out in all sorts of ways so that they don't disappoint anyone and risk being unloved.

Another part of The Labrador's unconscious story is an unrecognised element of pride. 'Look at how much I do for people. When I'm not there, everything falls apart. If I don't organise this networking event, or the exit teas or the baby showers, no one else will. Because I do it, I'm appreciated and loved.' This is, of course, untrue. There are others who can and will do it, but Labradors claim that space because it feeds their need to be loved and acknowledged.

Labradors don't consciously ask for what they want in the form of love, appreciation, recognition or acknowledgement. But they maintain the expectation of 'If I love you, you'll reciprocate at some point'. And when people don't, they're shattered.

The healthy Labrador

Labradors are love on two legs: they're warm and giving, and are always mindful of the feelings of others. Their best things in life are closeness, sharing, family and friendship. They're generally regarded as upbeat folk who lift the mood for others as they sprinkle love dust around them.

At their best, Labradors are self-nurturing, humble and gracious while supporting others. They have deep, lasting friendships, many of them dating back to early childhood.

Labradors have a rich sense of being in service to others and somehow know on an intuitive level what we each need most at any particular time. They'll be the person who will, years after you've emigrated, send a note to wish you happy birthday, or happy emigration anniversary. The Labrador is the person in the office who has a list of everyone's birthday and will send the balloons or organise the celebratory drinks. The healthy version of The Labrador will add their own birthdate to the list so that they, too, are celebrated.

Labradors at their healthiest are shining examples of the concept of servant-leadership, whether in the office or at home. They know who they are and the value they bring to the world. They're able to have the tough conversations with care. At the same time, they can ask for what they want or need.

The unhealthy Labrador: The Donkey

Both The Labrador and The Donkey are servants to man. However, while The Labrador gives of self unconditionally and feels exceptionally proud when they please their master, and will do more of the same to ensure the love lasts, The Donkey is known to be stubborn when it feels overburdened, and needs cajoling, love and attention before it chooses to move on.

The Donkey represents the willingness of The Labrador to take on the responsibilities of others that aren't theirs to carry. Typical beasts of burden, Donkeys will take on more and more, even when it becomes clear that they're carrying far more than they can cope with.

The Donkey does this because if they don't, who will love them? This highlights the martyr aspect of this personality type: 'I do so much and still they don't acknowledge me.' They're so busy loving and supporting others that they forget their own needs, and this leads to repressed anger and hurt for this type.

Donkeys feel comfortable offering unsolicited advice and can end up manipulating the person and the situation, braying the same tune, on and on. Donkeys are also known to offer flattery to great effect and can be successful seducers. They may be possessive of the people they love, holding onto them, wanting to keep them close and tight.

The Labrador at work

Because Labradors are driven by a desire to be loved, they've learned that one of the quickest ways to achieve this is to please people with their warm, generous, loving manner. Labradors are often service-oriented and can make themselves indispensable. Giving can be a subtle strategy to ensure their power or position.

They will try to lift the general mood, often putting on a happy face when they don't feel it. This can lead to their feeling resentful, or even angry, as the martyr-like 'I do everything for everyone' story makes itself known.

Labradors run the risk of dropping the ball in the tasks they take on, because their focus tends to be on human connection, so they find it difficult to make tough decisions.

Their instinctive action of jumping in to rescue one and all puts them at risk of burnout in the workplace.

Because they need to be loved, recognised and appreciated, Labradors find critical feedback really tough, even if the conversation is constructive and in their interest.

On one hand, they can be overly sensitive and try to hide their emotions at work; on the other, they can be forceful and seemingly unkind if they feel their needs aren't being recognised.

The Labrador in relationships

The Labrador is the parent who bakes for bake days at their child's school and who volunteers for the school fete day, the warm and loving mom or dad that all the other kids love and wish that their mom or dad was just like. The Labrador parent can, however, be the smothering type. Is it possible to love too much? Yes, when you don't allow your child to become a responsible person.

As life partners, Labradors are deeply caring, great listeners. They're attuned to their partners' every need: most often, before their partner has even asked for something, their needs are being attended to. The downside is that Labradors can become a martyr to their partners' needs, forgetting that they have needs of their own.

A LABRADOR'S STORY: LEARNING TO ASK FOR WHAT I WANT

Avril, a 59-year old personal assistant, recounted in one of our first sessions the memories of her being about 8 years old and realising how she could win friends by sharing the contents of her school lunchbox with them, or by bringing her special friends sweets or special gifts. A pattern developed: giving to get.

The most difficult aspect of the coaching for Avril was for her to own up to the manipulating ways of her type, which may have been unconscious at one point, but weren't any longer.

Avril told me how her entire family would come for dinner every Friday night. She'd be busy all afternoon cooking and decorating, and then serving the meal, even cutting her grandchildren's food into smaller bite-sized portions. When she finally sat down at the table, there was often very little left for her. She would say that she'd been around food all day and wasn't very hungry, even if she was ravenous.

Avril spoke of how, when she told her family that they shouldn't worry to help clear away the dinner mess, what she actually wanted was for them to help, and how resentful and sometimes angry she felt when they didn't.

We spoke of how Avril had to be clear in asking for help, in spite of the fact that she was sometimes overcome with deep concern that these bold requests would leave her unloved and uncared for.

Self-growth work

Possible areas of focus:

- Allowing yourself to receive.
- Saying yes to yourself before saying yes to others.
- Focusing on what you love.
- Recognising your value.
- Setting boundaries.

From a place of humility, recognise your own value

The work of The Labrador is a journey of respecting themselves for the incredible and loving people they are; of understanding they need not depend on others for validation; and of knowing that self-love is important for everyone but especially for a nurturer. Their journey is to learn that when they're at ease loving themselves, they invite others to love them in the way they desire and deserve.

There's a beautiful humility in carers when they're comfortable in their own skin, and how they're able to be themselves with everyone, from the CEO of a business to the waiter at their favourite restaurant. They have the ability to connect from a pure heart space and demonstrate that we're all interconnected and that there's value in each of us.

Self-check questions
Is this a loving thought or action towards myself?
Does this action demonstrate my humility or my manipulation?

Affirmations
My self-worth does not depend on being accepted by others.
Today I'm choosing to love me.

Work on saying no to others

'No' is not a word in the vocabulary of Labradors, who will often say yes when they mean no. And if they do manage to say no, they'll also give a thousand and one justifications for saying it, and hasten to add assurance that if that person 'can't manage without me, I'll pitch in'.

Self-check questions
How would it benefit me to say no?
Can I offer a half-hour instead of a full day?

Affirmations
I'm confident in my ability to say no.
I'm becoming assertive.

Work on saying yes to self

Being selfish isn't always a bad thing: it can be necessary and healthy. Think of the air steward who says, 'In the event of a sudden drop in cabin pressure, an oxygen mask will drop from the hold above your head. Secure your own mask before assisting others.' Labradors can work on recognising that they can say yes to themselves, and no one will think less of them or that they're being selfish. Putting on their own masks before helping another allows them to be more present to themselves and others.

Say what you need or want

To shift into a more powerful version of themselves, Labradors need to state what they need or want and, equally, what they don't. It's about making a clear shift to asking for help and not being the help.

Labradors need to learn that they're not being rejected if they ask for something and their request is denied. It's their request that's being declined, not them personally. They are still loved.

What we all tend to do in relationships is love the person in the manner that *we* want to be loved, for example, if receiving gifts is your 'love language', you'll be the bearer of gifts to all and sundry. Labradors especially should recognise how they want to be loved and ask for it, saying, for example, 'What I really need is a hug' or 'Can we talk this out? I need to share how I feel.'

Be mindful of your beguiling ways

'I love you, and I shower you with love and gifts, but in fact I do this in the deep hope you'll love me in return.' Giving to get is an aspect of the Labrador that's usually hidden from their conscious state. One of the toughest pieces of self-work for a Labrador is the recognition of this aspect of their personality.

Do a quick check before sending those flowers. Are you sending them with strings attached? Do you expect an effusive thank-you or a gift for your birthday a couple of days later? Do you send gifts to everyone? Is this your way of luring people in?

Self-check questions
Why am I saying or doing this?
What am I hoping for in return?

Affirmations
My intentions are honourable.
Gratitude is in the act of authentic giving.

A LABRADOR'S STORY: A LIFE IN SERVICE TO HIS SON

When John's son left home at 18 to study in another city, as many children do, John was deeply wounded. He became the martyr: 'I gave up my life for my boy and now he's left me and I never get to see him. Is this how he repays the sacrifices I made for him?'

John, like other Labrador types, repressed his darker emotions and instead kept up the shiny, friendly front. Instead of using this insight as an opportunity to speak to his son of his feelings of disappointment and rejection, he chose to remain silent.

Labradors will do anything, even to their own detriment, if there's a perceived need. This can make them feel possessive, but also needy, victimised, bitter or resentful. They forget boundaries and their own need to be independent. They're so attuned to serving others that they forget that it's not required to be liked in return.

Paths to greater success

Life lesson

Love can't be bought, nor does it depend on your capacity for giving. It's quite simple: love is yours unconditionally.

Emotional awareness practice

An example of emotional awareness might be that you noticed how you're feeling sorry for yourself because you're sick in bed and a friend hasn't called, whereas you always call and take her chicken soup when she's ill.

Step 1: Name the emotion

What are you feeling? Name the emotion.

Labradors may be surprised at the depth of their sadness, given that they might not have acknowledged it until now, or even repressed it for the longest time.

Step 2: Find the story

What's the story you're telling about yourself, the situation or the other person?

- *Nobody has noticed my contribution.*
- *I've been criticised.*
- *It's my fault.*
- *They take me for granted.*

Step 3: Reframe the story

If there was a neutral observer to this situation, what story might they tell? What's the different story that you're not seeing?

- *Am I mothering or manipulating?*
- *For the sake of who or what am I offering or doing this?*
- *Have they really ignored me? Is it possible they haven't seen my message?*
- *How might I benefit by saying no?*

Physical awareness practice

Labradors are feelings based, and their energy and attention are committed to connecting with people. Their great capacity for empathising with others can become a problem if they absorb the emotional state of others and lose contact with their own feelings and sensations.

The task of The Labrador is to focus on their personal needs, feelings and physical sensations. Doing so will help them create boundaries and separate their needs and feelings from those of others.

Labradors tend to breathe into the chest rather than the belly, and may feel cut off at the diaphragm. They can also hold their breath at times while waiting for a loving response. Do the breathing exercise recommended on <u>page 29</u>.

Language awareness practice

The language of The Labrador is often:

- ✗ *How can I help you?*
- ✗ *Let me do that for you.*
- ✗ *I do so much for everyone.*
- ✗ *I'm never helping again (until I do).*

How about a new refrain?

- ✓ *May I ask for your help on this project?*
- ✓ *I think it would be a great idea if we shared the responsibility of designing the menu.*
- ✓ *Instead of my jumping in and offering, can I check with you: do you need my input or help?*

 Thank you for asking, but I'd be able to assist only in the next week or so.

A LABRADOR'S STORY: I'M THE ONE THEY WANT

'Finding out I was a Labrador was really a confirmation of things I'd come to realise about myself over the years,' says Helena, a 55-year-old executive assistant. 'I always describe myself as a people person: I'm naturally drawn to people and am able quickly to establish intimacy with them. People turn to me for empathy, because they perceive that I care. They ask my advice and opinion on things. My work roles have consistently been as a support resource, assistant or coach.'

However, says Helena, 'I noticed that I often felt I wasn't being effective in a team, and I then blamed myself. During the first 10 years or so of my career, I was lauded as the heart of the team, while at the same time I was accused of being too emotional. My fear was that if I did stand up for myself, or I disagreed, I might be disliked or, worse, not loved.

'I was shaken when I read that The Labrador's deep fear is that they can't be unloved. I'd never seen it before but now I see how it has played out in my career. I've had to learn to stand up for myself to the point where I don't care if it means I'll be "unloved".'

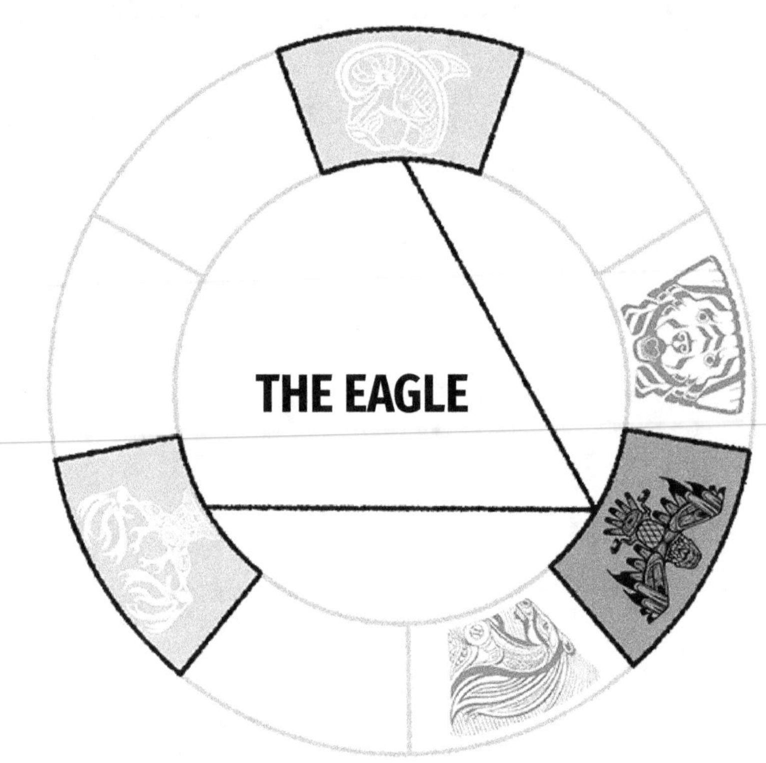
THE EAGLE

'Even the mightiest eagle comes down to the
treetops to rest.'
– *African proverb*

Well-known Eagles

Oprah Winfrey, Muhammad Ali, Will Smith, Lady Gaga, Tiger
Woods, Tom Cruise, Sharon Stone, Shania Twain, Deepak Chopra,
Tony Robbins, Arnold Schwarzenegger, Lance Armstrong, Ryan
Seacrest

Other names for the Eagle

The Performer, The Chameleon or The Competitive Achiever.

Are you an Eagle? Do you:

- Feel it important to be as efficient as possible to ensure you achieve your life goals?
- Try to be anyone to everyone – a true shape-shifter?
- Never stop working, to the extent that some people gasp at your capacity for work?
- Feel it's very important to be acknowledged for your success?
- Hide your failures or gaps in ability from others so that your façade of total success is unblemished?
- Know that people call you successful, and possibly even a role model?
- Carry perhaps just a hint of the snake-oil salesman?
- Oversell yourself?

The Eagle is represented as type 3 in the enneagram.

The Eagle can morph seamlessly into any situation or role. This ability is one they deliberately cultivate in their pursuit of success. Eagles have a very practical take on life and are willing to make sacrifices to achieve their objectives. Given their drive to succeed, they quickly realise one goal so that they can move on to the next. Life is all about demonstrating their success as their take is that only winners are recognised.

Eagles may find emotions messy, and feel that they get in the way of getting the job done. This doesn't mean that they're emotionless, however: it's just that they prefer to deal with emotions when they're ready, and mostly they're not ready.

Eagles feel a strong sense of worth from being recognised for their achievements. They talk about enjoying what they do, but it's not always the work they enjoy, but the race itself and the achievement of being first across the finish line.

Eagles wouldn't win any awards for being the best listening partners in town. They tend to move into their own headspace when people are waffling in conversation.

Triggers for The Eagle

- Not looking good professionally.
- Believing potential failure is on the horizon.
- Not receiving credit for their work.
- Sensing things are moving too slowly.
- Being undervalued or dismissed.
- Criticism or rejection of them personally, or of their success.

The Eagle's unconscious story: 'I can't be insignificant or worthless'

The greatest fear for an Eagle is being seen as a nobody, even if no one on the outside looking in would have a hint of this. Eagles are the world's doers and notably successful achievers. Maintaining this image is of paramount importance to them, even if they have to deceive themselves and others in the process.

Eagles prefer working solo so that they don't have to rely on anyone along the way. Success falls squarely on their own shoulders. But there's a cost. While Eagles focus mostly on the art of doing, they move away from their authentic self, and distance themselves from their heart space. To them, emotions are generally obstacles to their success.

The healthy Eagle

At their balanced and healthy best, Eagles are curious and adaptable. Trendsetters, they're charming and charismatic, and people want to be around them and bask in their success.

Eagles are comfortable engaging in meaningful relationships. They know they're acknowledged for the person they are and not for the riches they bring or successes they achieve. They've determined that their net worth doesn't determine their self-worth.

Eagles acknowledge there's personal work to be done to be in touch with their emotions, and that they can be vulnerable with themselves and others. They're working on being able to talk about their failures, with the focus shifting from avoiding failure at all costs to what may be learned in the process of failure.

Healthy Eagles recognise that it's possible to be more successful in life when doing things steadily and mindfully, rather than quickly and arrogantly believing they're the best. They're aware of the benefits of slowing down, of being present in the moment and of not having to be dazzling in every encounter. From time to time even star performers need downtime.

Eagles are quietly opportunistic in calculating the best path to success. They're open to hearing and valuing the opinions and perspectives of those around them.

The unhealthy Eagle: The Fox

Foxes are clever and resourceful. They have a hunting strategy, and an air of adaptability, underscored by a hint of wiliness and guile. All of these characteristics highlight their ability to win at all costs.

The Fox, like The Eagle, has the classic A-type personality behaviour: driven, ambitious and highly competitive. Foxes can be exceptionally stealthy in their approach to their goal and, if need be, will manipulate a situation to support their success. They may even become exploitative and opportunistic, as the need for success may drive them to do anything to maintain their reputation for success.

Foxes can be self-promoting and narcissistic. They have a tendency to blow their own trumpet while masking their lack of self-worth. By the same token, their need to avoid failure is so great that they're known to step away from a project rather than be part of something that has failed.

In its natural habitat, The Fox can not only outrun the pack, it knows how to throw people off its scent. Indeed, The Fox may appear to be manically driven, constantly on the go, as if trying to outrun failure. People may struggle to keep up with Foxes, which leads to a sense of irritation for the Fox, as their tolerance for the slow, or slow-paced, is low.

Relationships generally suffer when The Fox is in command, as they focus on the task at hand and, of course, successful delivery of the project, disregarding people and their emotions, including their own.

The Eagle at work

Be it losing or messing up a project or simply not coming out tops, failure is simply not an option for Eagles, who are determined to be successful at anything and everything they do. Being the star of the show is easy for Eagles, and holding this spot or leading a successful team is what Eagles consider their natural place. They tend to outshine others, and that's important to them.

The value that one Eagle sees in being the most successful CEO may be the same as another Eagle feels from being the best kindergarten teacher or yoga coach. Success is about being the best and being seen as having value and adding worth. It's not necessarily about the title.

Eagles tend to be straightforward; small talk isn't something they abide. Eagles need to be direct, and tend to move through life in the most straightforward and effective way.

Colleagues might find the behaviour of Eagles a little rude or disrespectful because as soon as they've contributed to a meeting, they tend to check out, reaching for their mobile or constantly looking at their watch as a way to tell everyone they're done and the meeting should be over.

Eagles may find themselves irritated by colleagues who spend what they (the Eagles) consider to be undue time fine-tuning the details of a project. Slowing down is difficult for Eagles, who're exceptionally task and goal oriented, and in each project there has to be a measurement or determination of success.

Eagles have an adaptive way of being in the world. They're tuned into and are exceptionally astute as to what their audience requires, and will morph themselves to suit every situation. This gives them the ability to assess a situation and reframe, refocus and realign a presentation midstream, ensuring a successful, slick delivery.

The Eagle in relationships

As a parent, The Eagle will be focused on ensuring their own success as far as their parenting skills are concerned, as well as ensuring the successful achievements of their child. They're the parent not in the stands, cheering along with all the other parents, but on the sidelines shouting for their kid to score the goal.

In a relationship the Eagle can be playful, creative, full of energy and supportive of their partner's success. On the other hand, in an unhealthy state, the Eagle would be overly focused on their own success and the achievement of their professional goals, and have very little to no time for the relationship or their partner.

AN EAGLE'S STORY: BEING THE BEST AT EVERYTHING

Throughout his school years, Graham, now a 34-year-old chief financial officer, tried his best to be number one at everything. He was able to achieve a number of big successes but, he says, 'I've always had a fundamental belief that there's more for me to achieve to be accepted. I always wanted to be the leader and I got there. But once I'd achieved this position, it wasn't about how I could make this position better but rather how I could achieve the next one. Later in life this played out as the need always to have the best, for example, if I decide to try a new hobby or sport, I had to have the best gear before I even knew if I'd enjoy it. Good gear guaranteed success.

'When I started working on my animal personality type, I realised that my ability to work with obstacles was due not to my resilience but rather to my determination to succeed at every task. Failure wasn't an option, and I didn't like to confront emotion but would rather delay or ignore it.

'I've now become more aware of my need for achievement and have realised that I need to slow down sometimes and enjoy the moment. I've come to accept that this need for achievement is key to who I am, and I've learned to question not the need but my motives behind it. I've learned to monitor the environment around me, as my constant need for success can lead to my neglecting other important areas of my life.

'For me as a business leader running large teams, finding my animal personality really opened my mind to how we can use diversity to a team's advantage. I realised that one of my passions was actually working with people, but I'd neglected the people for the sake of driving delivery and success. I was fortunate to be setting up a new team at the time of this work with Juanene, so I was able to change my leadership style completely. I worked on being inclusive, where my focus was on building a strong, open culture, based on collaboration and shared values, and I found that by doing this I was able to build a far better team and deliver much more.

'On the personal side I've also found ways to slow down and enjoy all aspects of life.'

Self-growth work

Possible areas of focus:

- Being present to everything that's happening in your life, not just your achievements.
- Recognising you're not your accomplishments.
- Unmasking your emotions.
- Slowing your pace through life.
- Investigating what else is possible.

Create stillness

Eagles are busy chasing success and wanting to avoid failure. They're constantly in motion. It's beneficial for an Eagle to consciously make the time to slow down, for example to create a practice of meditation or to engage in meaningful non-work-related conversation with another.

Self-check questions
What am I most afraid of when I sit in stillness with myself?
What might I learn to acknowledge about myself as I create a practice of stillness?

Affirmations
In stillness I connect with my inner strength.
Creating a practice of stillness enhances my life in many ways.

Speak about your emotions

Eagles tend to hold their own emotional space close to their chest and prefer to talk about what they do. Sharing their feelings with others will help other people connect more deeply with Eagles.

Part of the Eagle's daily journey of learning is to discover who they are behind their masks. This calls on them to be more open to emotion and to the practice of questioning themselves.

Self-check questions
What stops me from sharing my feelings with others?
What or how am I feeling?

Affirmations
When I accept myself for who I am and not what I do, I'm freed from the burden of needing the acknowledgement of others.
I'm able to connect with my emotions.

Become creative

For Eagles, finding and exploring their creative space is essential to learning to do something that has nothing to do with success, only pleasure. It could be picking up a guitar for the first time, writing a poem or the lyrics to a song, or trying a hand at baking. In any form of art there's neither success nor failure: beauty is in the eye of the beholder. When they give themselves permission to be creative, Eagles become more expansive in themselves.

Self-check questions
How did I express myself creatively today?
Where before have I been moved by creativity? How might I make that possible for myself?

Affirmations
Today I'm making the time to express myself creatively.
My creativity attracts brilliant ideas.

Work on humility

Humility isn't a word most would use about The Eagle. Eagles have a tendency to brag or speak openly of their own strengths or achievements. It's difficult for an Eagle to see that they're not their possessions or the work they do or the position they hold.

Eagles should spend time with people whom they would never deem as successful, resisting talking about themselves and rather focusing on learning about the other person – what makes them tick, not what they've accomplished.

Self-check questions
What might I learn that I didn't already know, by simply recognising who the person is, rather than judging them by what they've achieved? How can I reduce the words 'me', 'I', 'my' and 'mine' when talking to others?

Affirmations
I am who I am, not what I do.
A magnificent life is built on humility and success.

Watch your wily nature

Eagles need to acknowledge that they can drop easily into the sly Fox side of their personality, and then they'll do anything to achieve success. Their success can be achieved through being authentic and real. They don't have to be cunning to ensure their desired outcomes.

Examine 'what else?' scenarios

When Eagles are running from failure, they don't necessarily take a step back and look at other scenarios available to them. It's necessary for the Eagle to pause regularly and consistently during a project or intervention to ensure that the desired outcome is still achievable, as well as to consider other possible solutions to support the goal.

AN EAGLE'S STORY: PLAY TIME

Jonathan, a company director, would completely railroad his colleagues in the boardroom, in his need to outperform and outshine.

Once, a merger was on the table and someone present was going to lose their position in the company. This particularly dominant Eagle wasn't having any of that: he wasn't going to be the one to lose. Showing complete disregard for the others in the room, he gave nobody a chance to speak. His air of confidence and eloquence about his supposed abilities completely overshadowed the duping that was actually happening. He kept his job.

Afterwards, Jonathan was very clear in our conversation that he'd done the right thing for himself. 'There was no way in hell that I was going down with a sinking ship. Their inability to sell themselves was their undoing. I know my worth and it was the perfect opportunity for me to let the new people know how lucky they were in having me part of the new structure.'

Paths to greater success

Life lesson

To reclaim the truth that worth comes to you because of who you are, not because of what you do.

Emotional awareness practice

An example of awareness for an Eagle might be acknowledging how impatient they've become with the slower people on their team, or how upset they are that they and their team have been pipped at the post by another team.

Step 1: Name the emotion

What are you feeling? Name the emotion.
It might be a novel experience for The Eagle to own and articulate their emotions, whether they're betrayal, disregard or irritation.

Step 2: Find the story

What's the story you're telling about yourself, the situation or the other person?

- *I should be doing more, so that they notice me and my efforts.*
- *There's a quicker, easier way. Why can't they see that the end justifies the means?*
- *Nobody will find out and it really doesn't matter anyway.*

Step 3: Reframe the story

If there was a neutral observer to this situation, what story might they tell? What's a different story that you're not seeing?

- *In what ways have I been shape-shifting myself to suit the situation?*
- *How do I deceive myself?*

- *How do I avoid failure?*
- *What's the correct action in this moment?*

Physical awareness practice

Eagles tend to hold rigidity in the top half of their body and carry their pressure or tension in the chest and heart area. This makes them susceptible to heart attacks and a weakened immune system. Do the breathing exercise recommended on page 29.

Focus on breathing deeply into your belly rather than your chest. Allow the tension from your chest to open and soften. Let it flow into your belly and dissipate. Try to surrender as much as possible as you breathe out, letting yourself relax, and let go of any tension with every exhalation.

Language awareness practice

Eagles have a vocabulary that speaks to success, and seldom about emotion. Eagles may say:

✗ *Are we on track for a successful delivery?*
✗ *I'm ready for the launch, but I'm being delayed by inefficient people.*
✗ *There's no room for failure on this project, so let's make it happen, people.*

How about a new conversation?

✓ *Team, what do you need from me so that we can all succeed on this project?*
✓ *Before we hit 'go', what are some of the pitfalls you foresee on this project and how will we manage them?*
✓ *What might be the benefit to the team if I step aside for a while?*
✓ *How can I demonstrate heart-centred leadership today?*

AN EAGLE'S STORY: COLLECTIVE ACHIEVEMENT

Haseem, a 43-year-old senior leader, was always striving to stand out. He compared himself to others and cared a lot about what others thought of him.

'I built good relationships with work colleagues but sometimes I strained them as I focused solely on business and professional outcomes rather than balancing these with the wellbeing of the team and my relationship with others,' he says.

'I grew up in a family that valued financial wealth and status. I carried a deep fear of not being successful and being unable to look after myself and my family. I constantly feared being insignificant and useless.

'After understanding my personality type, I adopted some mantras that have helped me. These are "I'm willing to follow a meandering path to success", "I listen to understand" and "I don't have to be formal to be professional".

'I now focus a lot more on collective, rather than personal, achievement. I feel more at ease doing my job and leading others, as I'm not striving to stand out and achieve the step-up to the detriment of others

'I don't attach myself to a role, job or a title, but rather look at it as doing a good job and delivering as a team, realising that this will naturally lead to the growth of both my team and me.'

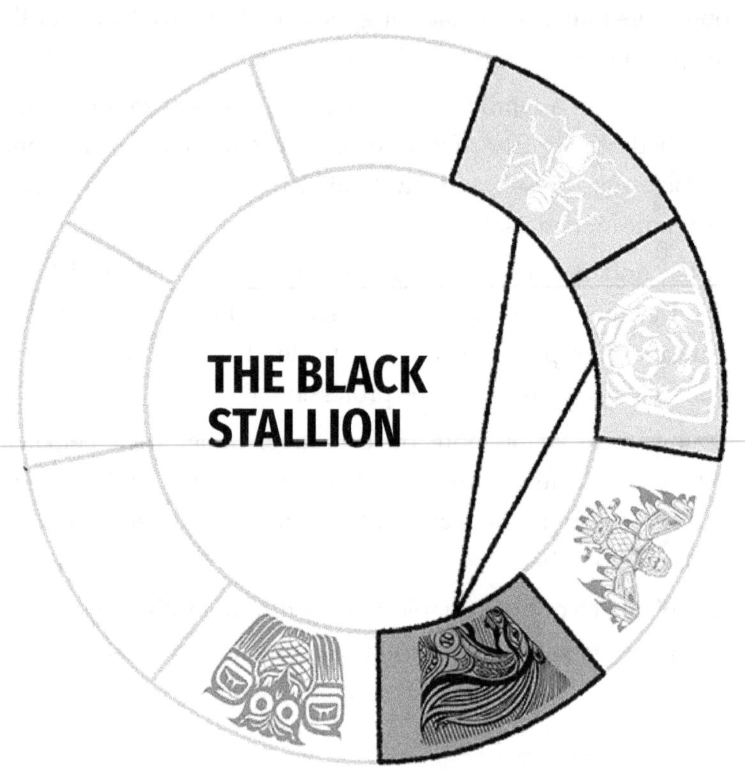

THE BLACK STALLION

'The wind of heaven is that which blows between
a horse's ears.'
– *Arabian proverb*

Well-known Black Stallions

Johnny Depp, Prince, Leonard Cohen, Cher, Sylvia Plath, Jackie Onassis, Alanis Morissette, Bob Dylan, Angelina Jolie, Amy Winehouse

Other names for the Black Stallion

The Individualist, The Intense Creative or The Tragic Romantic.

Are you a Black Stallion? Do you:
- Have a deep yearning to seek meaning?
- Feel intensely creative?
- Have a sense of grace and beauty?
- Have both strength and fragility on equal and opposite sides of the scale?
- Embrace all emotions, being comfortable with going deep and dark?
- Tend to be a drama queen?
- Constantly search for a space in which to belong?

The Black Stallion is represented as type 4 in the enneagram.

Black Stallions are intuitive, creative and emotionally strong. Their alternative name 'Intense Creative' aptly captures their inner and outer worlds. They're often labelled the drama queens of life due to the intensity of their emotional landscape – but it is this very intensity that makes them feel alive.

Black Stallions can be obsessed with being different or even unique. They have a deep desire to be authentic and are known for their individuality – yet they also badly want to belong. Because of this, they have a push-pull way of being in the world.

They're unafraid of emotions and, because they're comfortable with feelings, can be overly emotional or moody. However, because of their natural ability to be comfortable with emotions, they're able to support non-Black Stallion personalities in accessing hidden emotions and healing possible emotional pains. On the other side of the coin, the comfort Black Stallions feel when deep in their emotions puts them at risk of holding on to an emotion long past its sell-by date.

Black Stallions look for deep, meaningful relationships and show disdain for conversations or relationships that lack depth of emotion.

Triggers for The Black Stallion

- Being (or feeling) ignored.
- Feeling misunderstood or abandoned.
- Going against their sense of authenticity.
- Being dismissed, specifically when they're expressing emotion.
- Feeling they've been given insufficient time to attend to a need or emotion.
- Feeling they've hit a creative block.

The Black Stallion's unconscious story: 'I can't be without identity'

The Black Stallion's underlying story is that no one understands them because they're fundamentally different from everyone else. And because of this, they don't feel accepted or included, and may find it difficult to fit in.

Black Stallions deeply believe there's something missing in their life and in them, and this creates a sense of emptiness within them. When they look out into the world, everyone else appears to have happier, more fulfilled lives than they do. This external view into others' lives creates an unacknowledged envy in Black Stallions.

Black Stallions also find comfort in the melancholy of life, although they aren't always aware of this. When this mood takes hold, The Black Stallion will withdraw from the world and turn their focus inward, into their darker, more turbulent emotions.

The healthy Black Stallion

At their best, Black Stallions can be profoundly creative. They can be inspired, self-renewing and self-regenerating.

Black Stallions in this healthy state are self-aware, mindful of not only their feelings but their inner impulses. They can be sensitive to themselves and others. They're intuitive, gentle, tactful, compassionate, highly personal, individualistic and true to themselves, emotionally honest and self-revealing.

Black Stallions may have an ironic view of themselves and life. They can be serious but funny, vulnerable but emotionally strong. The quirkiness of Black Stallions can set them apart from others.

At the same time as wanting to be experienced and understood for being exceptional, Black Stallions also want to connect deeply, meaningfully and authentically. They have a huge capacity for courage to be themselves, to be authentic and true to who they really are.

Black Stallions are the people to consult when you're going through a rough patch in life. Their capacity for feeling makes them comforting to have around when others are working through difficult emotions.

Black Stallions are known to use their dress sense to express their emotions. When they feel anger, passion or love, they may wear red; or, because everyone else wears red to express these emotions, they might just wear green instead. When heavy with emotion, they may wear black – or they may pitch up in a rainbow of colours to express their individuality.

The unhealthy Black Stallion: The Basset Hound

The shadow personality of the Black Stallion has a melancholy and sadness to it, like the eyes of a Basset Hound. The Basset Hound is known as a clown dog, one minute crying in the depths of despair and melancholy, the next classic jesters.

The Basset Hound's referencing can be all about their feelings, thoughts and experiences, without regard for others. It's at times like these that people around them experience them as self-absorbed and overly dramatic.

Basset Hounds when bored can become a little destructive with their emotions, whether it be their constant bemoaning of their terrible fate in life or harping on how everyone has a far better life than theirs. Their emotions can flood everyone around them.

Basset Hounds feel shame and fatigue when they become absorbed in their feelings of inferiority, and may find it difficult to function. When life doesn't work out the way they wish and their plans fail, Basset Hounds can become self-inhibiting, angry at themselves or depressed. They may even alienate themselves from others, moving inwards and becoming removed from the people around them.

If The Basset Hound doesn't take the time to work through these negative emotions, they can fall into a deeper state of despair. They may torment themselves with deluded feelings of self-contempt. They may experience times of self-reproach and self-hatred, and allow themselves extremely gloomy thoughts. They will both blame others for their current state of affairs and drive away anyone who tries to help.

If left unattended, the emotional spiral may go as far as thoughts of self-destruction. Some may abuse alcohol or drugs to escape their intense feelings. Extreme actions and emotions, such as emotional breakdowns or suicidal thoughts and tendencies, can emerge.

The Black Stallion at work

Just because Black Stallions are usually artistic, don't for a minute box them into the arty world. Their creativity is demonstrated in every aspect of who they are, and they bring flair to any position or role they occupy. Passionate visionaries, Black Stallions make excellent entrepreneurs, teachers or therapists.

They hold a deep need to be authentic in everything they do.

They prefer to work with organisations and individuals who share support for authentic expression in the world.

Black Stallions are hyper-intuitive and will often understand the unspoken words in a meeting or around a boardroom table. As leaders, they can sense emotions and draw them out.

They hate and will rebel against repetitive, mundane things.

When results don't measure up, they easily become disappointed and tend to withdraw. Yet they come alive and are fully committed when they believe a project is worthy of their time and energy.

Black Stallions seek a personal, meaningful connection to their work and other people but, paradoxically, also fear they may lose their identity by being the same as other people at work.

Known to be self-absorbed and dramatic, Black Stallions can quickly fall into the trap of being a victim should they feel left out. They're extremely sensitive to rejection and may from time to time say they feel as if they don't fit into the team or organisation and are misunderstood. They may envy anyone who supposedly has it better than they do.

As they're known to be dramatic and sometimes overly emotional, people tend to tread on eggshells around them, never quite sure what emotional behaviour they may trigger.

They dress in ways particular to them, accentuating their personal style. Wearing any kind of uniform or following a dress code may be stifling to a Black Stallion.

The Black Stallion in relationships

As in other relationships, the Black Stallion in a personal relationship can be moody and overly dramatic, and equally carefree and playful. They tend to gravitate to life partners who're comfortable with their need to express their emotions, regardless of the emotion, as well as requiring a sense of belonging within the relationship.

As parents, Black Stallions tend to instil a love for all things creative in their children, whether that be baking, writing poetry or playing a musical instrument. They're deeply caring and can be great role models for children learning their way around emotional intelligence.

A BLACK STALLION'S STORY: UNIQUE ALL THE WAY TO THE BANK

Khanyisile was an anomaly in the somewhat sedate organisation she worked for in the financial sector. There was nothing staid about her at all, from her height, 1.86m tall, to her voice, which you could hear from the elevators booming across the open-plan terrain, to her dress – navy blue for who?

She always dressed differently (of course), and used her clothing to demonstrate to her colleagues, and anyone else who may notice, her mood or theme of the day or week. For her, it was a shout-out to all and sundry to notice her and the creativity in the rest of the team.

Given that it was her nature to disregard anything run of the mill, she'd been given the label of being a bit of a troublemaker.

'They brought me into this role because of my quirky and offbeat views,' she says. 'I told them that I'm not a yes-girl and that I'd challenge their outdated ways of doing business, and they said it was exactly what they needed, and now I'm being penalised for who I am and what I was employed for. How does that work?'

We spoke about what it was that she wanted to achieve for herself in her role, and how she might still achieve that in her unique way, albeit somewhat muted. For example, instead of wearing a floppy hat with a flower garland that would be more suited to a horse derby, perhaps she could wear a colourful scarf?

We also looked at ways that she could support others emotionally rather than being the one who constantly demanded emotional recognition, given her drama-queen tendencies.

Self-growth work

Possible areas of focus:
- Owning that you're unique and don't fit stereotypical patterns.
- Become more emotionally resilient.
- Valuing your intuition.
- Accepting what is, rather than focusing on what isn't.
- Seeing yourself as part of, not separate.

Love your uniqueness

Black Stallions need to learn to love who they are – to love their differences and not envy what they think they're missing out on by being who they are. They should embrace the fact that they avoid ordinariness, and equally be comfortable with it, for in the mundane they may find another aspect of themselves. Black Stallions should be open to seeing in themselves those attributes they covet in others.

Self-check questions
Do I see in me that trait that I envy in her?
How might my uniqueness bring joy to me and those around me?

Affirmations
I acknowledge that I have in me what I see in others.
I love all that is me, my ordinariness and uniqueness in equal parts.

Focus on the good stuff

By focusing on positive emotions and using more positive language, Black Stallions can come to think positively about themselves and others, and focus less on comparing themselves unfavourably to others. When they can focus on others rather than themselves, they can start moving away from their self-centred drama.

Self-check questions
What's a different and more impactful way of experiencing this right now?
What might be a positive in this situation?

Affirmations
I am comfortable with a range of emotions and I value all emotions.
My emotional stability brings a sense of ease to my life.

Set goals and deadlines

Black Stallions dislike mundane structure or boundaries. It's important for them to notice, though, how a balanced sense of structure brings balance to life. Black Stallions should set up boundaries, whether to friendships or tasks at hand, and should aim to set goals, timelines and fixed deadlines, especially for tasks they think are boring.

Self-check questions
What is it I want to move towards with purpose?
What does success look like for me?

Affirmations
I achieve my goals, and they support me and my dreams.
Structure benefits me in ways I have yet to realise.

Curb the drama

When Black Stallions' emotions run amok, they flood the people around them. There's always space and time for emotions, yet it's beneficial to learn to contain emotions and not let them leak out inappropriately, for example, not resorting to childlike sulking. To achieve this, Black Stallions should develop a method of identifying and naming particular emotions.

Self-check questions
What is this emotion I'm feeling right now?
Can I park this emotion temporarily so I can focus
on the matter at hand?

Affirmations
I am more than my emotions.
I let go of the need to be temperamental.

Find brain-heart balance

We all have three 'brains': our head (which manages logic and information), our heart (which manages feelings and emotions) and our gut (which manages our sense of ourselves in the world). Black Stallions need to become adept at accessing the head and gut brains. By recognising and using both, they'll find more balance in the area of thinking, feeling and action. If a Black Stallion can harness all three brains, they're downright formidable.

Use your intuition

Black Stallions tend to be highly intuitive around unspoken matters, using their gut to work better with people. When working in a team, Black Stallions can tap into this to great effect.

A BLACK STALLION'S STORY: APPROPRIATE EXHIBITIONISM

Lola was an incredible artist. She was, in her own words, 'not a paint-by-numbers mail-order artist', and felt that her art was important and necessary for all women. The problem was that she wasn't making any money from her showings. People would come to her exhibitions but there were no red 'sold' stickers next to any piece of art at the end of an evening.

I popped by her studio to get a sense of her art and to try and understand what the reasons may be behind the lack of sales. The graphic depictions on the canvases in front of me took my breath away, and I immediately understood why she held onto her belief that her art was important and necessary – and I equally understood why there were no red stickers.

Each of the 10 giant pieces depicted women in various states of physical abuse, graphically rendered and leaving nothing to the imagination. Lola had been abused in a recent relationship and still had the physical scars on her body, and her healing process was laid bare on the canvases. The dramatics of her personality and the pain of her abuse were overwhelming for her audience and potential buyers.

'I agreed, over time, to take on commissioned pieces of art where the subject matter was in line with my values,' she says. 'Each piece was still unique within itself. Six months later I held an exhibition showcasing some of my commissioned pieces, some abstract work and two of the smaller pieces from my earlier exhibits. Both of the smaller pieces sold, and I picked up two new commissions.'

Lola was able to be authentic and true to herself in her commissions, while at the same time holding true to her abuse and bringing awareness of it to society, only in a somewhat tempered way.

Paths to greater success

Life lesson

To appreciate in the present moment what is; to accept yourself as you are without having the need to be unique or special.

Emotional awareness practice

An example of awareness may be that you find that your emotional dam floods its banks and there's an emotional deluge that drowns you and those around you.

Step 1: Name the emotion

What are you feeling? Name the emotion.

Black Stallions may notice that they're overwhelmed by emotions. Articulating specific emotions may allow them to take the necessary action, such as naming their anger and/or letting their partner know how they're feeling and what led to their being angry.

Step 2: Find the story

What's the story you're telling about yourself, the situation or the other person?

- *People just don't get me.*
- *Why can't I have what they have?*
- *I've lost all my creativity and have nothing to offer the world.*
- *Nothing is working in my life.*

Step 3: Reframe the story

If there was a neutral observer to this situation, what story might they tell? What's a different story that you're not seeing?

- *How have I focused my attention and energy on what was*

missing, and how can I change this perspective?

- *In what ways do I experience a sense of longing or envy, and how is this impacting me?*
- *Do I feel pride in being special or unique and do I focus too intently on this?*
- *In what ways have I felt misunderstood and what can I do about it?*

Physical awareness practice

The big work of The Black Stallion is to ground themselves in reality and not focus only on emotion. Look at working on experiencing what's happening in your body, rather than indulging the bigger story centred primarily on emotions.

Are you able to focus on your breath and the physical sensation in your body? It will help to ground you and connect you to the vitality of your instincts.

Meditation and breath work are great practices. Each of these will bring you a sense of groundedness and open the space to step out of your emotions. Do the breathing exercise recommended on page 29.

Another practice is to go for a walk and just feel the rhythm of your body.

A third is to ground yourself by taking your shoes off and standing on the grass or on a beach. Think of yourself as taking root, feeling grounded and connecting to the earth itself.

Language awareness practice

The Black Stallion feels comfortable speaking their truths and their full range of emotions but not everyone is as emotionally literate as they are, and some may find such conversations overwhelming. When this happens, the Black Stallion's words may be:

- ✗ *Why can no one see how deeply I'm suffering?*
- ✗ *Being in corporate is killing my need to be authentic and to engage in meaningful conversations.*

* *I wish that I could be just like her; how I envy her lifestyle.*
* *They wouldn't understand how their decision to exclude me from the project has triggered my fear of abandonment.*

How about using another approach?

✓ *Jack, may we speak about your comment in the meeting room yesterday and the impact it had on me?*
✓ *I can see that speaking about deep emotions makes you feel uncomfortable.*
✓ *I'm going to use that trigger of envy as a springboard to making stuff happen in my own life.*
✓ *Team, I felt completely overlooked and ignored when you excluded me from the project. May we chat about how we might manage this moving forward?*

A BLACK STALLION'S STORY: I LIVED A CRAZY-BEAUTIFUL DRAMA

People describe Renee as very intense and at times quite dramatic person. 'I was always deeply insecure about myself, feeling that no matter what I did, nothing was good enough,' says this 45-year-old entrepreneur. 'I paid more attention to the negative aspects of myself than the positive.

'I often got lost in stories about life, finding myself reminiscing about past encounters or partners, and wishing I had the chance to go back and do things differently. It just always felt as though something was missing, no matter how much I actually had.'

When it came to her personal relationships, men were always drawn to her in a 'crazy-beautiful kind of way'. 'I became like the dangerous game they took a chance on playing,' she says.

'I found myself most uncomfortable when things around me were working and made issues where there weren't any. I found myself looking for everything that was wrong about my partners and letting them know about it. They didn't stand a chance at their attempts to love me. I always knew exactly what to say that would push them over the edge. I pushed them to hurt me back. Then I made them suffer even more. I lost a lot of people this way and learnt many hard lessons.

'Now, through working with Juanene, I've become aware of all this about myself, and have made huge efforts at recognising when my story is at play. I work now on seeing the wood instead of just the trees. I aim to take responsibility for all aspects of my life rather slipping into blame and anger.

'I believe I'm much less intense now and more centred, and I'm certainly more content. There's a general flow and acceptance about my life that I didn't have before understanding myself.

'I believe becoming a parent was also paramount in a lot of the changes I've made. I want my daughter to understand that behaviour and perception are choices we make.

'The area of life that is still a big stretch for me is my relationships. However, I experience and express gratitude often, and am able to see now when I'm playing into my stories.

'I tell myself that life just isn't as serious as it feels. I have fun, laugh and play. And nothing is personal or about me – neither the good nor the bad. I just go about my day, focusing on what makes my heart feel good and trying to see what I have, not what's missing.'

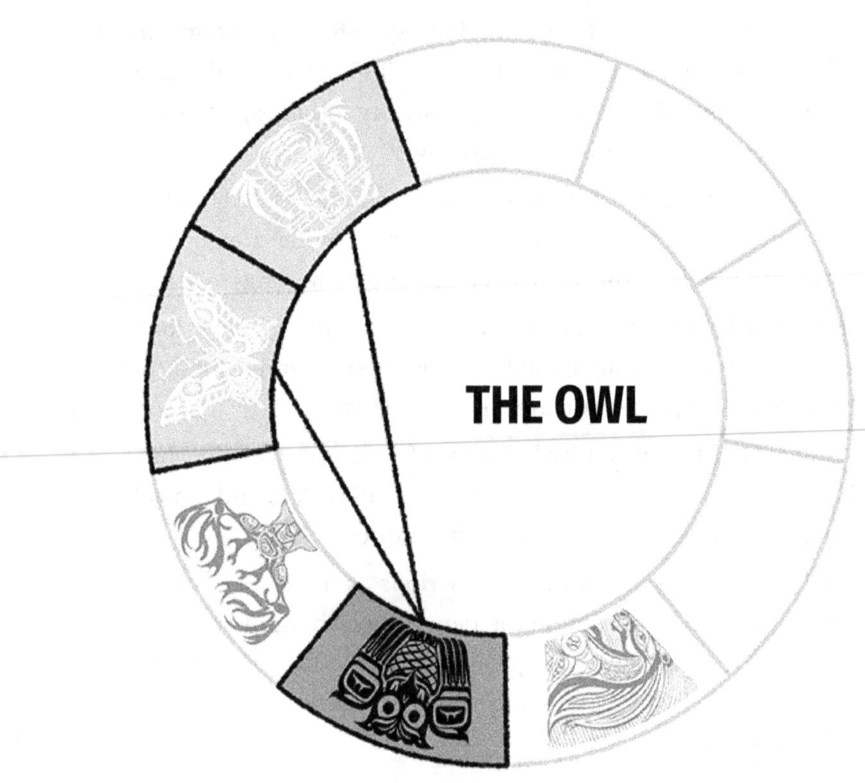

THE OWL

'A wise old owl lived in an oak; the more he saw the
less he spoke.'
– Nursery rhyme

Well-known Owls

Bill Gates, Mark Zuckerberg, Stephen Hawking, Julian Assange,
Stephen King, Lily Tomlin, Kurt Cobain, Eckhart Tolle, David
Lynch, Jodie Foster

Other names for the Owl

The Investigator, The Thinker or The Quiet Specialist.

Are you an Owl? Do you:

- Not tire of your own company?
- Have a deep desire to understand, to be the specialist in
  that thing that has grasped your attention and piqued your
  curiosity?
- Hold on tightly to your sense of privacy?
- Hoard your time, energy and knowledge?
- Tend to connect with people whom you deem to be on a
  par with you intellectually?
- Find emotions draining?
- Compartmentalise with ease (which, to a large degree,
  supports your being in the world)?

The Owl is represented as type 5 in the enneagram.

Owls desire to understand everything about their area of
specialisation, and have a general curiosity about the mechanics
of everything.

Possibly the most recognised introvert of all the animal types,
they tend to have a social awkwardness about them and are more
comfortable with their inner thoughts than they are with fellow
human beings.

To a degree, because of their desire to go it alone, they have to work on their emotional intelligence and emotional connectivity with people so that they allow the world and potential suitors in.

This defence against emotions also protects them against being flooded by the emotions of others.

One of their coping mechanisms is to compartmentalise everything, from the food on their dinner plate to their relationships. They would never, for example, talk social stuff in the office, and vice versa.

Owls dislike surprises and function far better knowing the rules of engagement, such as timelines on a project, or the time they're expected to be at dinner.

Triggers for The Owl

- Not being recognised and respected for their knowledge of a particular matter.
- Disregard for their boundaries.
- Breaking confidence.
- Being micro-managed.
- Invasive behaviour.
- Interruptions.
- Emotional drama.
- Being taken unawares or surprised.
- Unpredictability.

The Owl's unconscious story: 'I can't be dependent on others or be exhausted.'

Owls believe they have to be independent and that they can't rely on anyone else. This extends to their area of expertise, where they find it difficult to trust others' input. The paradox of needing to live life on their own is that they become exhausted, which happens to be their second-biggest fear.

They have a desire to understand life's deep intricacies and, since they tend to be loners, they fill their emotional emptiness with knowledge. They're known to hoard information or knowledge rather than share.

Owls can become so engrossed in learning and seeking knowledge that they forget there's a world outside their inner space. Because of their desire to do things on their own and to be self-sufficient, and their need for personal space, they can find themselves alone and lonely, isolated from people and from their emotions.

The Owl prefers to study emotions rather than feel them, as emotions are messy, and feeling them would mean they would have to let down their intellectual guard and step into a heart space that they can't control with their minds.

The healthy Owl

Owls are mentally alert and curious, often with a searching intelligence. Highly independent and eccentric, in their healthy state they've developed their own way of engaging in what would otherwise be considered by them to be an emotional world.

In their quest for knowledge, Owls may become experts in a subject, attaining mastery and producing extremely valuable, innovative and original work. Owls can become visionaries: because of their desire to understand, they may make pioneering and revolutionary discoveries, with new ways of perceiving and doing things.

Owls are observant, perceptive and insightful. It's as though nothing escapes their notice. They have high levels of concentration, to the point of becoming engrossed in their subject to the detriment of their personal relationships.

Owls at a healthy level of self-awareness can bring their visions into the world with courage and conviction. They recognise the value they bring to a conversation or meeting when engaging in the world and connecting with others. At this level they develop a sense of adventure and can throw caution to the wind while they explore new opportunities.

Owls have a dry sense of humour and, when they feel

comfortable in their own skin, delight the people around them with their approachability mixed with ribald, witty ways.

The unhealthy Owl: The Hamster

The shadow aspects or behaviours of The Owl are similar to the hoarding habits of The Hamster. Hamsters begin to fear a lack of inner resources, such as time and energy, and detach themselves even more from the outside world, believing that by being detached or separate from the world they'll be able to hold onto what they perceive to be these limited resources.

At times like this, Hamsters further detach from emotion, fearing they'll drain or deplete themselves and their already diminished energy. Hamsters move even more into their cognitive brain and hoard information without integrating it into their lives, for example, reading about taking charge in meetings and then not practising any of the tips in a meeting.

They become reclusive, and can embrace a state of anarchy, going against established rules or laws. They may become extremely eccentric in the way they do or say things or the way they dress. They may even reject and repulse all social attachments and connections with others.

The paradox of all this is that, as much as they fear to depend on anyone else and/or become exhausted, they become fatigued from treading the hamster wheel of their own limiting actions.

Hamsters can be without a significant other or an intimate relationship. This doesn't mean they don't want one but they'll forsake it to further their intellectual way of engaging with the world.

The Owl at work

In the workplace, Owls have a natural tendency towards collation of data, a sense of intrigue in getting to the nugget of the matter, or a desire to be the specialist in a particular field. The Owl would be the chief data officer of an organisation.

Owls are professional. They don't like drama and messy

emotions. They prefer clear, concise communications. They tend to be more comfortable with data than with humans. They manage emotions by separating them from the rest of their world.

Although they may compartmentalise things, they are visionary and pioneering in their thinking. An Owl exemplifies our need as humans to understand how things work.

Owls experience an urgency to dive deeply, to delve into and understand the finer workings of something. This desire can make them seem unapproachable because they're focused more on facts and figures than casual chitchat.

They find it difficult to share their knowledge, ideas, intellect and themselves, as, in their unconscious story, this very knowledge sets them apart. Owls believe in their superior knowledge, which can make them appear supercilious and arrogant. It's a no-brainer for them to withdraw from the world in pursuit of their next intellectual adventure.

They also choose to isolate themselves because they feel that people and their emotions are messy. The Owl's comfort zone is cognitive engagement, and they feel they need to conserve their energy and avoid reliance on others. This is why you may find an Owl colleague sitting quietly on their own in a corner of the office – if they could, they'd have their own office with a door they could close when they chose.

The Owl can be a phenomenal team player, bringing expert thinking and strategic insights to conversations and matters at hand. Equally, team members can find it exceptionally difficult to engage with Owls when they detach themselves emotionally, and sometimes physically, and ignore team relationships.

The Owl in relationships

The Owl parent would better engage with, say, a 5 – or 6-year-old than a toddler – the younger child would take too much energy for The Owl to manage, given the emotional outbursts, whereas they could engage on a more 'adult' level with a child who can reason. They'd be the parent who'd help with research projects but not the bake day.

As a partner, The Owl would need a lot of personal space and alone time, and would find it exceptionally difficult being with a needy, clingy significant other. They'd also benefit from a partner who's understanding of their cognitive approach to emotions, for example, when asked how they're feeling, The Owl may respond with a cognitive reply rather than knowing how they truly feel.

They're also not social butterflies, so their partner needs to understand that they, the partner, might be attending a number of social events on their own.

AN OWL'S STORY: RED FOR NO-GO, GREEN FOR GO

JP was a senior manager within data analytics for a large organisation. He mainly kept to himself most days. He was at his desk when his teammates arrived and he left long after the floor was emptied of people and noise.

During a big company re-design, open-plan seating became the new floorplan. He was horrified. His worst nightmare was unfolding before him. He quickly devised a plan to manage the noise, the intrusions, the bleeding emotions of others. He bought the best-quality sound-cancelling headphones he could afford and told his line manager he'd be wearing them during working hours.

Then he created a traffic-light system using flags. When the red flag was raised at his desk, no-one was to approach him unless the building was burning. The orange flag meant approach at your peril and with a damn good reason for intruding on his space. And the green flag meant you could approach.

It was only when JP received his first performance-review feedback that he sat up and paid attention to what was being said about him, not only by his peers and colleagues but by his leadership. The general consensus was that he consciously isolated himself from the team, and was therefore not a team player. They felt that he didn't contribute to the team debates or discussions.

'The work I did with Juanene was determining a strategy of visibility while still holding true to who I am,' he says. 'I was visible – everyone knew the 'dude with the headphones' – but no one heard my voice.

'I agreed to speak up once at each meeting, to voice my opinion and offer my insights, and to challenge viewpoints around the table.

'We also worked on my engaging more with my colleagues – to be curious as to who they were and how they might share common interests. I learned to soften my guard around my time and my need for independence.'

Six months later JP was promoted. His promotion feedback mentioned his insightful contribution to the team.

Self-growth work

Possible areas of focus:

- Being mindful of exhaustion.
- Engaging with the world rather than isolating.
- Sharing your expertise with the world.
- Becoming more aware of your body and emotional centre.
- Connecting with others from a heart-centred space.

Watch your energy levels

Core fears of The Owl are to be dependent on other people and to be exhausted. The paradox is that they try to do everything themselves and end up being exhausted anyway. So Owls need to be mindful of their exhaustion, and of how their energy is depleted.

Self-check questions
Am I aware of my body being sluggish?
Am I eating healthily?

Affirmations
I'm reaching out and asking for help.
I take quality care of my body and my health.

Be generous

Owls have a tendency to be hoarders with their knowledge – their unacknowledged weakness is avarice with resources. They need to work on being open, and giving generously of themselves, and of their intellect and knowledge. They can bring the most inordinate value to a team or organisation but they need to share the good stuff.

Check in

Set up a practice to check in with yourself at least once a day. Did you move away from your desk, even if it was to make a cup of tea? Did you engage with your colleagues during the day? What did you do differently today at the team meeting?

Be free within yourself

A challenge for Owls is to be spontaneous, to engage with people around them, to let their hair down and let loose, so they need to try to engage in practices that they've decreed a waste of time. Turn on your warm glow. Allow people to experience you as the witty, intelligent person you are. Consciously switch off the cool-white light that makes you appear cold and standoffish.

Own your skills

Given the breadth and depth of your knowledge, speak up. Sit in the power chair. Use language that we can all understand. Allow us to see the value you bring to the conversation, to the organisation. Let us learn from you.

Are you compartmentalising?

It's important for Owls to recognise when they move into a state of compartmentalising everything. This need to compartmentalise becomes more pronounced when Owls are stressed, as it allows them to separate themselves from hard stuff like emotions and being present in life. For Owls, it's easier to be more concerned and engaged with cerebral happenings.

AN OWL'S STORY: LEARNING TO ACT ON THE SPUR OF THE MOMENT

For Janet, the concept of spontaneity was absolutely alien. If she was taken by surprise, it felt as though her world was being rocked and her life was being turned upside down. For her, spontaneity was depleting of energy, and she felt that if people around her acted in a spontaneous way, they would invade her privacy and she'd be left exhausted.

'It was one of the biggest challenges I'd ever accepted when, in my coaching engagement with Juanene, I took on the challenge to experience spontaneity,' says this 36-year-old tax-compliance officer. 'Initially I earmarked a day a month on which my family was allowed to be spontaneous for me. On the designated day, they would spontaneously decide where we were going for dinner, and the destination was always a big surprise.

'I absolutely hated it. Surprises just aren't my thing. I would feel exhausted by the end of the meal, simply because my sense of discomfort of the unknown was so great.

'It took me many months – in fact, close to a year – before I could spontaneously invite people over for dinner, or go with my daughter to the movies an hour after she'd suggested it.'

Paths to greater success

Life lesson

To reconnect to the vitality of your life force and your heartfelt feelings, realising that ample energy and resources are available.

Emotional awareness practice

An example of being aware of your default pattern is noticing a sense of being overwhelmed when a colleague puts you on the spot to answer a question, when you feel you have insufficient information and a roomful of people are hanging on your every word.

Step 1: Name the emotion

What are you feeling? Name the emotion.

Owls might find this step difficult simply because of their disconnection from their moods and emotions. Try locating where you're experiencing the sensation in your body, for instance, if your stomach has tightened. Next would be to articulate the emotion behind the sensation, for instance, 'I'm tensing up because I'm unsure of what they're about to say. I'm feeling unsure.'

Step 2: Find the story

What's the story you're telling about yourself, the situation or the other person?

- *I feel invaded. Don't people recognise the signs for privacy?*
- *Why do people break confidence? How can I trust them?*
- *I feel completely blindsided by his action.*
- *How am I supposed to be ready at the drop of a hat?*

Step 3: Reframe the story

What story might a neutral observer to this situation tell? What's a different story that you're not seeing?

- *How might I communicate my need for boundaries?*
- *Not everyone breaks confidence. Whom can I trust?*
- *How do I explain to my colleagues that I battle answering on the fly?*
- *Was Phumlani aware that I felt blindsided? How do we work together moving forward?*

Physical awareness practice

Owls tend to be stuck in their heads, so they benefit from slow breathing, bringing awareness down into their bodies. They may unconsciously hold their breath to avoid feelings or sensations that seem scary or overwhelming. This can constrict their vitality and keep the energy in their head.

Do the breathing exercise recommended on <u>page 29</u>.

Allowing the breath to drop lower into their body offers a new kind of security. Breathing into the belly will develop their capacity to be more grounded. Breathing into the chest will open space for both their personal feelings and their empathy, with more possibility of a heart connection with others.

Yoga or pilates are very liberating for Owls, as are long walks on the beach or promenade.

They're very sensitive to sound and touch, and they would benefit from massage.

Language awareness practice

Language for The Owl may sound something like:
- ✗ *I'm not going to last long here – they don't respect my privacy.*
- ✗ *All this emotional drama is exhausting. Can't people contain themselves?*
- ✗ *This is the exact reason that I don't rely on people. The quality of the research is pathetic.*

✗ *Don't people understand that I need to prep beforehand? I'm not the slapdash artist.*

How about a new refrain?

✓ *How do I tell my colleagues that I'm a private person and ask that they respect this?*
✓ *I'll limit my time in the canteen to once a week: that way I don't have to listen to his constant drama.*
✓ *Perhaps I didn't make myself clear – what might I have missed?*
✓ *Can I ask my manager for a schedule that highlights all upcoming meetings so that I can prepare?*

AN OWL'S STORY: ME, MYSELF AND I

Dalia had always been a thinker. For this 35-year-old social entrepreneur and CEO, some of her strongest memories of childhood were sitting alone in a quiet corner with a notebook or a sketchpad, doodling and letting her mind wander for hours. 'I loved asking myself existential questions and allowing my mind and my body to float into my imagined universe,' she recalls.

'My happiness was always my quiet time alone, with only my notebook, my novel or my laptop, and time to just be. In my early 20s, I thought that made me a bit weird. I looked at peers who seemed to socialise so seamlessly all the time and I felt forced to be more outward. I tried changing myself to be more extroverted and I found myself tired and unhappy.'

Dalia's appetite for information enabled her to move at a young age into a senior position at an investment bank but she knew that wasn't the career she wanted.

'At 28 I decided to start a social enterprise, and I thought the only way to do it was to partner with people who'd already been entrepreneurial. That was the hardest, most expensive, most draining mistake I made on my journey. I realise now that I had a preconceived idea of what a successful entrepreneur should be: extrovert, a networker, a people person. I didn't perceive myself to be any of those things.

'After working with Juanene, I realised that introversion is powerful. By allowing myself space and quiet time, I tend to be more comfortable and confident around people. I don't have ongoing capacity for people and, to get the best out of me, I need to give myself space on either end of challenging interactions.

'I respect that feeling is my weakest centre of expression. I know if I don't take the time to quieten my mind, I can become reactive. I know that presenting a veneer of confidence and direction is exhausting.

'I'm much more aware of the impact of that strain and I now try more deliberately to manage it. I'm open with my team about my capacity and let them know when I need a day of minimal contact so that I can be left with my thoughts.

'I love that I'm a deep thinker. I love that I can think through mazes of information and create a picture that no one else can see. I love that I don't have to be the loudest voice in a room but can still be respected for what I have to say. I love that I'm creative.'

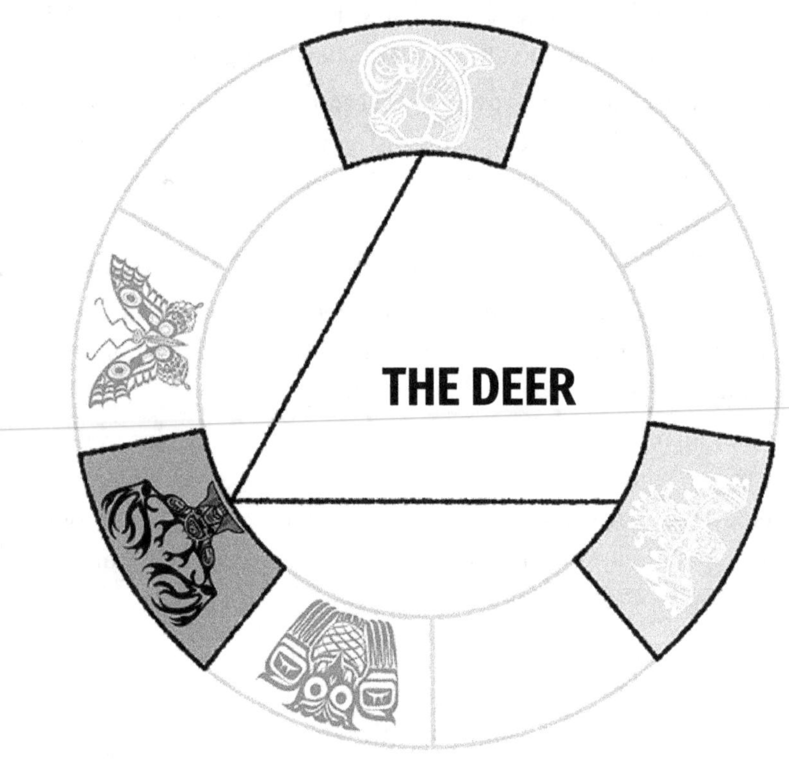

THE DEER

'Every morning in Africa, a gazelle wakes up; it knows it must outrun the fastest lion or it will be killed.'
– Christopher McDougall

Well-known Deers

Katie Holmes, Marilyn Monroe, Eminem, Chris Rock, Mike Tyson, Tom Hanks, Diane Keaton, Jay Leno, Bruce Springsteen, Julia Roberts, Jennifer Aniston

Other names for the Deer

The Loyal Skeptic, The Devil's Advocate or The Troubleshooter.

Are you a Deer? Do you:

- Consider yourself brain-driven and use this trait to anticipate problems?
- Seek solutions and establish rules and procedures to create a sense of security?
- Exhibit intense loyalty to people and situations where you've established your sense of safety?
- Mask fear and doubt by being warm in nature, or by following the rules, or (at the other extreme) by charging head-first into the perceived danger?
- Have a tendency to suffer analysis paralysis while you determine the safest next step?
- Tend to see catastrophes in all situations?

The Deer is represented as type 6 in the enneagram.

Scepticism of people, places and even the world at large is The Deer's natural manner of engagement. Deers apply a cautious approach to life, and are the best, most natural scenario planners, relying on their ability to sense risk and manage multiple possible outcomes and measures.

They are among the most loyal people you'll encounter. Their sense of loyalty is immense once they've established that it's safe to be your colleague, your partner or your teammate.

The Deer will unconsciously keep up their guard, waiting for that one slip in human behaviour. When it comes, their worst fear will be realised: they are indeed alone in a threatening world.

While some Deers are more cautious in their ways, experiencing a 'caught in the headlights' effect and avoiding decision-making or accepting tasks, there are also those who call up physical or intellectual strength and rush headlong into imminent danger, almost as if head-butting the situation will reduce the fallout.

It's their natural tendency to disbelieve almost everything until they've gathered enough information to give them a sense of relief and a map of the way forward. This doubting trait inevitably impacts their ability to make decisions for themselves and for the people for whom they care.

Triggers for The Deer

- Criticism or judgement of their sense of anxiety.
- A lack of reliability, predictability or consistency.
- Any situation where trust is broken.
- Being rushed – they don't like being put under pressure to come up with an on-the-spot solution.
- A lack of genuineness and warmth.
- Abusive use of authority.
- Being told that they're imagining something or to calm down.

The Deer's unconscious story: 'I'm alone in a threatening world'

Given their need to feel safe in a threatening world, Deers are always alert to potential danger. They're the first to notice irregularities and discrepancies, whether in conversation or in behaviour, and prepare themselves for danger which might not occur.

Deers may look for a sense of belonging with an individual or group, and in that feeling of safety they're able to show up as courageous, grow their sense of self-esteem and know that they have the ability to manage whatever life throws at them.

Rules and regulations bring a sense of security to The Deer, enabling them to manage the unknown and feel that there's a safety net should things go wrong.

There's also a Deer type that meets danger head-on as opposed to fearing it. For example, as opposed to being afraid of bungee-jumping and not partaking in it, they would jump off the highest and most terrifying bungee point, almost in defiance of any potential danger.

In the realisation and demonstration of inner strength, and inner knowing, they tap into a deep reservoir of stillness and faith, and an ability to recognise the benevolence of life and people.

The healthy Deer

Deers can be self-affirming, self-trusting, trusting of others and independent, yet interdependent and cooperative in equal parts. They can be truly courageous and demonstrate admirable leadership skills, expressing themselves in rich, flourishing terms. They have a deep sense of humour and are known for their quick wit.

They're loyal to family, friends, tribe or team. They're also great community builders, responsible, reliable and trustworthy.

In moments of crisis, Deers are calm. They've already assessed all possible threats, so when issues do arise, they're ready to take mindful action.

Deers work for the common good of people or society, and are comfortable doing so under the radar, without fanfare. They believe that when people band together, they can accomplish much more than any solo attempt to change the world.

The healthy version of The Deer is courageous, determined, outspoken and able to draw from a sense of inner calm and balance.

Because their natural desire is for accuracy, safety and meticulousness, their work satisfies the most exemplary standards.

Deers aren't crazy about pressure. They need time to think and plan; they have to scan and map all possible solutions. It's unwise to request one possible option from them, and don't put them on the spot – they find that type of request unsettling.

The unhealthy Deer: The Rabbit

In their unhealthy state, Deers are like Rabbits caught in headlights, distrusting themselves and others, behaving in a guarded manner, and projecting their own worries and concerns onto others. It's no wonder, then, that the people around them can become suspicious and guarded about them.

In this state of being captured, held hostage by fear, The Rabbit can become exceptionally sarcastic and defensive, panic-stricken and volatile. They might blame others for what is, or isn't, happening in their world, or, perceiving themselves as defenceless, look for a stronger authority to resolve problems.

Rabbits may become disparaging, berating others and sowing division. If they feel persecuted in any way, they may act irrationally by lashing out, thereby bringing about what they fear. They may become fanatical about thoughts, feelings or fears, expressing themselves with violence.

Rabbits procrastinate. They worry about all those external factors that can potentially go wrong, and they freeze. They can also vacillate between being clingy, emotionally reactive and defiant.

Rabbits may exaggerate possible and impending threats, becoming rigid about what's acceptable and what isn't, and dogmatic as to 'this is the way things get done around here'.

Because they're acutely aware of impending danger and the ways to manage it, they can sometimes create threats and potential dangers that don't exist.

The Deer at work

Deers have incredibly analytical minds and excel at logic, reason and abstract thinking. They're skilful trouble-shooters. In an office environment, they would be expert risk analysts or crisis-management specialists.

They like to work from a secure and known space, whether on their own or in a team. Determining loyalty and safety is key to their being able to function fully in their role or surroundings.

It takes some time to gain the trust of The Deer, and even when you have, they'll test you occasionally to ensure that you're still safe.

Deers are great team players. They want to be connected to, and supported by, their colleagues, and to foster a sense of belonging.

They can appear organised and responsible, but this is largely as a result of mapping out their own anxieties and all eventualities so that life can be trouble-free and predictable. They're calm in a crisis and foster the feeling of 'you can rely on me'.

On the flip side, since Deers constantly worry about what can go wrong, they often second-guess themselves, and they can unconsciously create an unsettled atmosphere for others, and elevate fears and concerns in the people around them.

Deers may procrastinate, freezing when they feel they don't have answers and/or don't know what to do next.

Deers feel they must always be prepared for any eventuality. For example, their PowerPoint presentation will be saved in a Dropbox file and backed up on a USB stick, and probably also sent to someone else for safekeeping. Prior to speaking, not only will they check the audiovisual equipment, they'll probably also have their own portable speaker and projector just in case something goes wrong.

The Deer in relationships

As parents, Deers would worry about every possible danger that might befall their child, and to a degree would stop their children from partaking in certain activities because of perceived potential dangers. This could lead to the child not developing a healthy sense of independence as they become afraid to try anything for themselves.

On the other hand, Deers could demonstrate courage for their children, given their ability to face danger head-on.

As a partner, The Deer can be suspicious and sceptical, for example, wondering why a partner has brought them flowers and what they're hiding or have done wrong. On the flip side, however, when they learn to trust themselves, to have faith in themselves, and to have faith in their partner and in the relationship, they're deeply loyal, warm and caring.

A DEER'S STORY: LEARNING TO LET GO OF THE PARENT STRINGS

Peter was finding it exceptionally difficult being a normal parent to his 9-year-old daughter, Annie. His wife had died eighteen months before, and he'd come to realise that he hadn't been engaged in a day-to-day way with Annie's schooling activities and had chosen to spend his time being concerned about their financial security. Now he was faced with a dilemma: should he allow Annie to attend a school outing or not? He was leaning towards her not going.

'I thought about all the things that could go wrong,' he says. 'The bus driver might not be competent. The bus could break down. The venue was in a part of town that I considered unsafe, which meant that there would be unsavoury characters lurking about. There were thirty children and only one teacher accompanying the group, so how was the teacher going to be able to be aware of where every child was at all times?'

Peter and I took each of his concerns and looked to other possibilities and how he might manage them. In the end, Pete volunteered as an aide to the teacher and accompanied the children on their outing.

'I did also ask the bus company for proof of the driver's licence, and I spoke with the venue managers, and arranged that they put up security on the perimeter of the property.'

Self-growth work

Possible areas of focus:

- Recognising that the only security you need in life comes from yourself.
- Building courage to move away from self-doubt.
- Learning to trust with a greater sense of ease.
- Creating space between your fears and yourself.
- Setting challenging, audacious goals.

Tame the fear

The Deer has a core fear of fear itself. They have a fear of being alone in a threatening world. The work is to differentiate between what is a real and necessary fear, and one that's perceived.

Deers have a heightened awareness of potential mayhem and constantly anticipate a threat or danger, where the imminent danger is usually far less than they expected if even real. When they calm their sense of anxiety, they recognise they have more choices than they initially thought.

Self-check questions
Is this fear necessary and true?
How might I remain calm in this situation?

Affirmations
I trust myself.
The world around me is safe and I am safe.

Check in with yourself

Interrogate the sense of fear and the story around the fearful situation. Look for the positives in the conversation instead of only determining what's going to go wrong.

You know that you can rely on yourself, you know that you're courageous, and it's time to remind yourself of this.

Up your heart rate

Deers hold a lot of stress in their bodies as they're constantly hyper-vigilant. Adrenaline, also known as the 'fight-or-flight' hormone, and the stress hormone cortisol flood our bodies in stressful moments. Any form of cardio exercise that will raise The Deer's heart rate to a healthy level, such as running or swimming, will enable them to release some of the adrenaline and cortisol in their bodies.

Know you're brave

Remind yourself of your courage, and of previous times you've demonstrated this courageous nature to yourself. You do have it in you. Pause for a moment, breathe, and take a determined step away from fear towards courage.

Identify other emotions

Build awareness around the emotions other than fear that you feel. For example, learn to differentiate between doubt, anxiety and fear, and how you might engage with each of them differently.

Have a plan

Focus on a specific outcome rather than on everything that may go wrong along the way. Once you've determined your goal, find the most direct route to achieving it: the fewer steps, the fewer opportunities to get caught up in worry.

Find your tribe

Deers like to find a tribe to which to belong, whether at home, in the office or on the sports field. They're exceptionally loyal when they know that the tribe has their back. They can then relax a lot more and focus on possibilities rather than failings.

Self-check questions
Do I feel connected to, and safe with, this group of people?
What is it that I want from a tribe and what am I willing to
do to find it?

Affirmations
I support my tribe and my tribe supports me.
I have a sense of belonging.

A DEER'S STORY: DIGGING DEEP

Jen, a newly qualified graduate who'd just entered the corporate work space, was finding it exceptionally difficult, second-guessing her every move as well as those of the other people in the small team. The perception her boss had about her was that she wasn't ready for the corporate environment, as she appeared to be too timid and unsure of herself, and he mentioned that unless things changed he wouldn't be offering her a fulltime role at the end of her probation period.

'Juanene and I worked together mapping out what my desired outcome was for my probationary period: what I needed to learn or upskill myself in, and what my concerns were, and whether they were real or perceived,' she says. 'We also looked at what the most practical and easiest steps were for me to take to ensure my successful appointment at the end of the trial period, and how I might see this as a growth opportunity and not that people were trying to catch me out. And I wanted to connect with my teammates a little more, and slowly build up a sense of trust with them.'

Jen's probation period was extended post the initial three months for another two months, and she was finally offered a permanent position in the team. 'It was success, one mindful step at a time,' she says.

Paths to greater success

Life lesson

To reclaim trust in yourself, others and the world, and to live comfortably alongside uncertainty.

Emotional awareness practice

Awareness might, for example, be that you're noticing fear has so immobilised you that you're unable to see what other solutions or possibilities may exist.

Step 1: Name the emotion

What are you feeling? Name the emotion.
Are you feeling worried? Is it anxiety, panic or terror?

Step 2: Find the story

What's the story you're telling about yourself, the situation or the other person?

- *It won't work.*
- *I don't have sufficient options available to me.*
- *They've broken my trust and I can't work with them.*
- *They don't share the same values as I do. I don't feel safe on the same team.*

Step 3: Reframe the story

What story might a neutral observer to this situation tell? What's a different story that you're not seeing?

- *What would it take for this project to get off the ground?*
- *If I gave myself dedicated time to consider the matter, would I be able to come up with another approach?*
- *How do we collectively understand trust, and what are the behaviours associated with it?*

- *Have I shared my values with the team and, equally, why they're important to me?*

Physical awareness practice

Deers tend to carry a lot of muscular tension and rigidity. For them, the task is to develop safety within themselves instead of relying on other people to provide this for them. Their journey is to move from fear to courage, supported by becoming centred and grounded in their body.

Develop an ability to notice when your alarm system kicks into a 'flee or freeze' response. Breathing into your belly will help restore calm and reduce your sense of anxiety. When you find yourself overthinking, worrying or holding your breath, return to the practice of steady breathing.

Sometimes all that's needed is a simple walk in nature to calm your thinking, your body and your turbulent emotions.

Do the breathing exercise recommended on page 29.

Language awareness practice

Your language may sound something like:

- ✗ *I'm feeling alone and unsupported.*
- ✗ *I'm so worried about what might happen at the meeting tomorrow morning.*
- ✗ *They keep rushing me for a decision and it's impossible for me to think.*
- ✗ *Who does she think she is, trying to throw her authority around like that?*

How about a new refrain?

- ✓ *My team and peers have my back; together we'll make this happen.*
- ✓ *Even though I'm concerned about the outcomes of tomorrow's meeting, I know that I have all the necessary information to support my point of view.*
- ✓ *If I tell my colleagues that I require a certain amount of thinking*

time, they're more likely to understand my irritation at their constant sense of urgency.

✓ *What conversation can I have with my boss to enable her to understand the impact of her leadership style?*

A DEER'S STORY: CORPORATE BULLYING NEARLY TOOK ME DOWN

Liezl, a 42-year-old senior manager, acknowledges that she has a serious look and an upright walk that may intimidate people. But, she says, 'I also have a bubbly personality with a great sense of humour. I choose to be part of the positive flow of life and tend to motivate and encourage people. I can clown around quite a bit and have a lot of acquaintances due to this.'

Liezl says she's considered by many to be 'way too deep and analytical'. Due to this, she says, 'I've generally been a loner and find I can relate to very few people. Those to whom I can relate are the ones who find me refreshing and can consider and understand how I view things.'

'I've had a very successful career, but I've been subjected to corporate bullying twice by management. The bullying was subtle and covert, and I found it exceedingly disconcerting to transition from being embraced to being insulted and criticised all the time. My self-confidence was broken in both instances, but I was determined not to allow my feelings and circumstances to harm my performance or compromise what I brought to the table.

'In the first instance, I remained bold and wouldn't back down. In the second, I chose not to fight back but started looking for another job. I felt like a coward by being silent, which was more frustrating than fighting a losing battle.

'I feel internally immobilised when exposed to abuse of power and when I'm unsafe, but I don't carry my challenges on my sleeve, so nobody really knew what I was going through. I was fearful, stressed, tense and anxious, and doubted myself and my abilities. I was extremely demotivated and frustrated.

'Since I started working with Juanene, I focus more on my thoughts and the impact they have on my body. I'm actively trying to focus more on what could go right and not everything that could go wrong. I remind myself of my strengths and am celebrating my gut because it's so accurate.'

THE BUTTERFLY

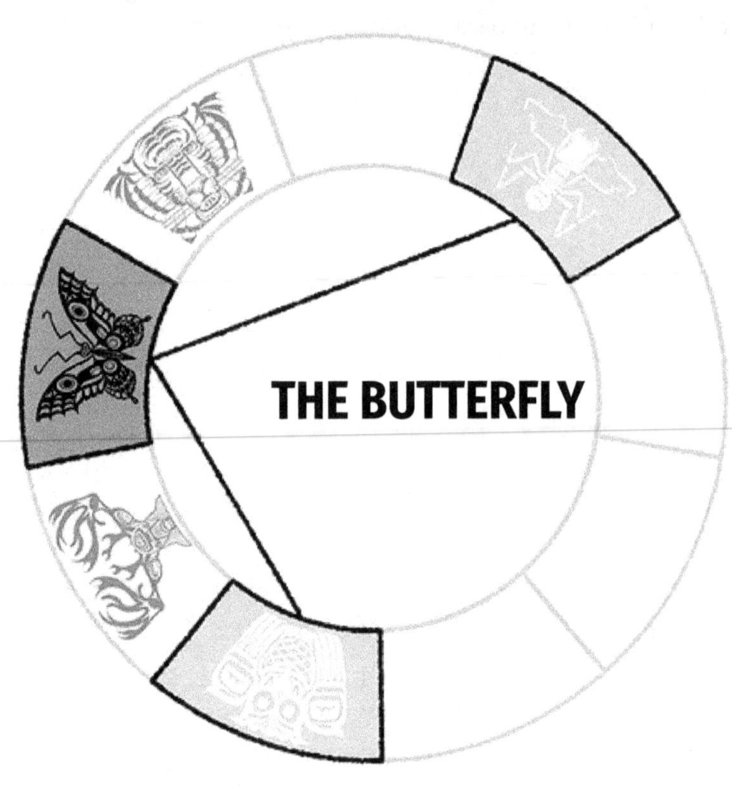

'A butterfly thinks itself a bird because it can fly.'
– African proverb

Well-known Butterflies

Robin Williams, Simon Cowell, Mick Jagger, Timothy Leary, Goldie Hawn, John F Kennedy, Bette Midler, Britney Spears, Sacha Baron Cohen

Other names for the Butterfly

The Dreamer, The Enthusiastic Visionary or The Dilettante.

Are you a Butterfly? Do you:

- Find it difficult and tiresome to be present in the here and now, preferring to pay attention to whatever new delight is calling your name?
- Mask your pain, sometimes even avoiding it at all costs?
- See life through rose-tinted glasses, as the eternal optimist?
- Have a restlessness about you, which you channel into your excitement of life, engaging in a plethora of ideas, people and events?
- Have a positive and upbeat disposition, so people around you wish they had your life (although what isn't seen is your escapism from tough emotions, avoidance of having roots, skimming of life)?
- Fake it until you make it?
- Tend to be a hands-off leader, one focused on innovation rather than implementation?

The Butterfly is represented as type 7 in the enneagram.

Butterflies have a gluttonous desire to stuff themselves with every pleasure and gratification possible, seeking pleasure in an array of delights and subjects with no desire to be a specialist in any. This serves to support their aversion to boredom and the experience of being boxed in.

Innovative, optimistic and future oriented, The Butterfly flits from one experience to the next in an attempt to avoid pain or emptiness. From one adventure to the next, they flutter, fast-talking, spontaneous, versatile and excitable.

Butterflies will often have a host of unfinished projects on hand, and part of their growth journey is to slow down, to plant and grow their ideas.

Of all the animal personality types, Butterflies are best at handling the vast amounts of stimuli and change that characterise our modern-day world.

The Butterfly is known to avoid negative emotions and rather focus on reframing them as positive. Although this may seem a good thing, the reality is that life should be balanced, and it's important for Butterflies to immerse themselves in both painful and joy-filled emotions and experiences.

Triggers for The Butterfly

- Experiencing anything boring, run-of-the-mill, mundane or unstimulating.
- Feeling as if they don't have options, or are hemmed in, controlled or limited in any shape or form.
- Being in the presence of negative people.
- Not being heard.
- Being told what to do.
- Working with people who aren't friendly and approachable.
- Having to spend too much time focusing on problems or negative issues.
- Unjust criticism.

The Butterfly's unconscious story: 'I can't be limited in any way. I can't be in pain'

The Butterfly's silent story is the constant nudge they feel to be in movement, specifically away from being controlled, boxed in or feeling pain. They don't accept the mundane, whether it's a person, experience or event.

This deep-seated urge keeps them constantly on the go. They feel that if they sit or stand still for too long, their worst nightmare will be realised: the boredom of life will consume them. They're good at winging it and going with the flow.

Butterflies have a need to experience everything that life has to offer, and more, and in excessive quantities, because they fear they might never have another opportunity. They crave as many options as possible, anything that's pleasurable, new or interesting.

Butterflies live for the heady experiences of life and instant gratification, which can lead to an addiction of sorts for the next high of life.

Exceptionally impulsive and light-hearted, Butterflies live with exhilaration; they're versatile and can turn even the ordinary into a major celebration. The Butterfly is like the eternal child never wanting to grow up or grow old, and instead experiencing life as a constant party of streamers and balloons.

Butterflies steadfastly believe that life is beautiful, even when the stench of it threatens asphyxiation. They're unable to recognise harsh realities.

The healthy Butterfly

Butterflies are divergent thinkers, and masters at connecting ideas and people. They're nimble in their ability to integrate and process information. Although they're known as generalists, they're also often accomplished achievers.

Healthy Butterflies can focus on the structure and processes that support the completion of a project, slowing down for long enough to experience life one bite at a time and to savour each moment.

They acknowledge their rose-tinted view of the world and to some degree set down the spectacles and see life for what it is: up and down, happy and sad. And in their healthy state, they're able to experience and speak of tough emotions like sadness. They're also able to recognise that what they need in life is not outside, but within themselves, and that the next adrenaline high will bring not long-lasting joy but rather a shortlived sense of euphoria.

There's a sense of sobriety about the healthy Butterfly: they're able to be present in *this* particular conversation, *this* particular project, *this* particular moment.

The more The Butterfly accepts and settles into what they have rather than focusing on what they don't have, the more dedicated they can become to accessing their innate creativity.

The unhealthy Butterfly: The Monkey

The unhealthy Butterfly is like a Monkey, chattering endlessly, swinging from idea to delicious idea. There's no real goal in mind, just an unconscious drive to be busy, to remain in a state of distraction. Dozens of trees each offer an abundance of enticing fruit for this monkey-mind to chase and feed on. As The Butterfly's core fears are being controlled and boxed in, and feeling pain, their Monkey selves constantly run, skip and jump, chasing the delights of life.

In their desperation to subdue anxieties, Monkeys may become impulsive and juvenile. They don't know when to stop and can be offensive, abusive, depraved and debauched, avoiding reality and wallowing in pleasure to excess. They're also known to spin out of control, experience erratic mood swings and act compulsively.

If The Monkey continues without addressing trigger issues, they finally run out of energy and feel controlled, hemmed in and panic-stricken. In this emotional state, they may fall into deep depression and despair.

Projecting a state of being on a constant high, ebullient and effervescent, Monkeys may worry that people don't take them seriously.

The Butterfly at work

Butterflies are the most extroverted of all the animal personality types. They're great storytellers, entertaining, engaging and compelling.

They're known for being big-picture visionaries, multitalented leaders and colleagues. Because they do so many things and generally do them all well, they tend to be generalists rather than specialists. They have vivid imaginations and innate abilities to inspire, innovate and disrupt, mobilising all those around them to a common purpose. They seem to have an unlimited capacity to dream beyond what's thought possible.

At their most distracted, however, they typify the Jack of all trades, master of none, which can lead to their being seen as somewhat flaky. Because of this, they run the risk of people dismissing them and their abilities.

They also have a propensity to look only at the lighter side of life, and not recognise that there will be pain and sadness in equal proportion to joy and happiness: don't expect The Butterfly to sit down and chat to you about your emotional distress and turmoil if you're unwilling to let them tell you how to look at the positive side of the situation and how you're so much better off for this having happened.

The challenge for The Butterfly at work is the need to recognise that their growth happens when they stick with one or two projects at a time, starting at the beginning and moving through each step all the way to the end, even when it all becomes constricting and boring. Recognising structure, process and order would afford them a wonderful sense of freedom.

The Butterfly in relationships

The Butterfly parent is a child's version of a best parent, flitting from face painting to baking to a movie, all in a day. As parents, Butterflies are as childlike as their children, delighting in all the joy-filled delights life has to offer. They wouldn't be the disciplinarian and their children might find this difficult, as the child might find they themselves instituting boundaries for their own sense of security.

As life partners, Butterflies can be flighty and somewhat

emotionally unavailable. They might tire you out with their social calendar and engagements. 'Runaway brides', Butterflies enjoy a relationship while it's carefree but the minute it becomes serious and they're starting to feel boxed in, they're known to do a runner.

A BUTTERFLY'S STORY: SLOWING DOWN TO ONE IDEA AT A TIME

'How long do I have to sit still and quiet? And what happens if I bump into a sad memory?'

These are the questions Thulz, a 33-year-old creative director, asked when she began working with me. She started with one minute – a whole 60 seconds – of mindfulness a day. She set her alarm three times a day and simply sat still and checked in. All she had to do at these times was pause her day and become mindful of her body, of what she was thinking and what she was feeling. Six months into the coaching, she can manage a comfortable half an hour of mindful exercise.

For Thulz, the 'monkey-mind' was a curse. 'I had so many ideas that my head hurt, but none of them materialised into anything more than doodles on a page. With Juanene, we spoke of the concept of contemplation, of slowing down to be present to one thought, one idea, one project at a time, and of how a discipline might support the slowing down.

'To simplify the practice of contemplation, we linked it to an existing habit. Each morning before getting ready for work, I spent five minutes writing down my top three goals for the day, and every Sunday afternoon, after lunch with my parents, I spent 10-15 minutes noting what was to be achieved in the week ahead.

'The combined practice of structure and contemplation allowed me the space to bring a number of my ideas to life.'

Self-growth work

Possible areas of focus:
- Working on completion and follow through.
- Paying attention to emotions.
- Spending time alone.
- Slowing down, savouring life, one sip at a time.
- Asking yourself what you're running from.

Be still

The core fear for The Butterfly is to be controlled and constricted. It's why they constantly flit about chasing life's delights.

The work for them is to slow down, go inward and feel the pain – to experience the hard emotion rather than reframing into a positive, for example, grieving the death of a close friend or relative and not saying, 'But they had a good innings' in a way that deflects having to feel the sadness of loss.

The deeper work of being still is to be present in the moment and the reality of the situation. Butterflies need to be physically, mentally and emotionally present. The learning path for them is to show sobriety to what is, not to be drunk on the highs of what might be.

Self-check questions
What benefit would I experience if I slowed down?
What am I feeling? Is this my standard go-to feeling or a new feeling?

Affirmations
I'm happy to be still and present.
I let go of the need to be busy.

Practising mindfulness

Mindfulness might be defined as the ability to pause between a trigger and a reaction. It's also creating a sense of stillness, a pause in the present moment, a focus on one matter, one thought at a time.

Self-check questions
Where is my focus: the future, or the here and now?
Am I focusing on one thought, one conversation at a time?

Affirmations
I have a deep appreciation for the wisdom of silence.
When I'm present and mindful, it allows me to tap into my inner guidance system.

Quality versus quantity

Butterflies love to live life to the absolute fullest. Their task is knowing when enough is enough. What's required is the art of discernment: learning which invitations to decline, which projects to turn down, which events to skip. It's being satisfied with a glass of champagne rather than chasing a magnum.

Self-check questions
Am I sipping or gulping life?
Can I decline this invitation, given that I've got four other events today?

Affirmations
I'm grateful for what I have.
I'm discerning in my life choices.

Following through

Following through and completing tasks takes attention and effort from The Butterfly, who's easily bored and wants to move to the next excitement. Two ways to do this would be to create clear and accountable deliverables on a project, and to do the boring work first.

Self-check questions
Have I seen this project through to the end?
What story am I telling myself about this being boring?

Affirmations
I mindfully focus my attention.
I successfully follow through and deliver on projects.

Facing the more difficult emotions

Butterflies have a sense of apprehension when they see pain heading their way, and have no qualms turning their backs and running from emotions such as fear or sadness. But learning comes not only from upbeat emotions in our life but through our embrace of the full range of emotions available to us.

Self-check questions
What is the story I'm telling myself about this pain?
How might I engage with the emotion?

Affirmations
I'm safe in working with my pain.
I'm able to engage with all my emotions in a safe and healthy way.

Speak less and with more impact

Butterflies are chatterboxes and tend to speak quickly, which dilutes their message and authority. When they come from a space of leadership, part of the work for them is to be more specific in their communication so that it lands with gravitas.

Self-check questions
What's the message that I want to communicate?
How might I say this succinctly and specifically?

Affirmations
I speak clearly and with impact.
Listening more allows other voices in the room to make themselves heard.

Work on a system

Often Butterflies have so much going on that they tend to see frameworks, structures or reporting lines as confinement, and so avoid them. But they flourish if they put systems and processes in place that help them shine. Structure with deadlines and targets focuses their output. Without these they tend to become lost.

Self-check questions
How might the structure of this process support me?
How might time conspire with me?

Affirmations
Structure supports my innovative thinking.
With each deliberate step I take, I move closer to realising my vision.

A BUTTERFLY'S STORY: FINDING FREEDOM WITHIN BOUNDARIES

Mercedes is a well-known and highly recognised artist, working on commissioned pieces only. Her artwork graces the walls of homes and organisations around the world.

'I approached Juanene shortly after an exceptionally lucrative contract had been cancelled due to my twice moving out the delivery date,' she says. 'We explored what it was about this particular project, the client and the timelines, and it turned out that the subject matter reminded me of my late mom, and when I stood in front of the easel to start the piece of work I was overcome with sadness, and it was easier to set the work aside and find a happier project to work on.'

The other insight was that the more Mercedes focused on the very tight timeline, which she'd agreed to, the more controlled and constricted she felt, and with that came a sense of anxiety and panic, and an inability to be creative on her canvas.

'We set out a framework where, moving forward, I could consider timelines before just agreeing to them with clients, ensuring that I gave myself enough time that the deadline felt expansive and not restrictive.'

And, where a project reminded Mercedes of a sadness in her past, I suggested she perhaps play upbeat music while painting, or that she spend some time considering how she might actually work through her own sense of sadness.

'Working with Juanene, I realised that certain processes, frameworks and structures actually gave me more freedom to do what I wanted to do.'

Paths to greater success

Life lesson

To accept all of life in the present moment, with all its pleasures and all its pains.

Emotional practice

An example of awareness might be one that's accompanied by a strong emotion, such as when you're hurting from a painful experience and you notice the urge to run.

Step 1: Name the emotion

What are you feeling? Name the emotion.

Butterflies feel at ease experiencing the more positive emotions like joy or gratitude, whereas naming an emotion like hopelessness or sadness might be more difficult.

Step 2: Find the story

What's the story you're telling about you, the situation or the other person?

- *Why on earth can't we work on multiple approaches at the same time?*
- *This is positively the most boring meeting of my entire life.*
- *Being retrenched is a fabulous opportunity for her to start her own business – why's she so angry at me for saying that?*

Step 3: Reframe the story

How might a neutral observer to this situation relate this story? What's a different story that you're not seeing?

- *How might focusing on one approach benefit me, the team and the project?*
- *If I participated in the conversation, would it make the meeting*

more engaging?

- *How do positive options and opportunities absorb my attention and energy so that I don't have to pay attention to those emotions that I label as negative like pain or sadness?*
- *What conversation do I need to have with my boss so that he understands my need to work flexitime?*

Physical awareness practice

The challenge for a Butterfly is to become, and remain, grounded in their bodies. Their energy pattern is up and out, where it should be down and in. Exercise is a good way to bring a Butterfly into their physicality.

Do the breathing exercise recommended on <u>page 29</u>, and when you experience a sense of calm, draw your attention up the length of your body and check in around your knees, hips, belly, shoulders, neck and jaw. Loosen the tension as you move upwards. When you're ready, bring your attention back to the room you're in, and mindfully stand up and end the breathing exercise.

Language awareness practice

Language for The Butterfly may sound something like:

- ✗ *My partner has just moved into my apartment – little did I know how hemmed in I'd feel.*
- ✗ *Why does everyone focus on what can go wrong? What about what's working?*
- ✗ *This is why I prefer working on my own – having to wait for people to deliver drives me to distraction.*
- ✗ *All work and no play make Jack a dull boy, so let's party.*

How about a new refrain?

- ✓ *I'm going to have a chat with Sphetho and explain my need for girl-time, me-time.*
- ✓ *Am I ignoring the potential pitfalls so that I don't have to worry*

about my own pain?
- ✓ *What conversations do we need to have about meeting deadlines?*
- ✓ *How can I create a sense of balance for myself?*

A BUTTERFLY'S STORY: CHASING THE SUNSET

For Davina, a 44-year-old life coach, her 20s and early 30s were all about chasing the next exciting experience. 'The result is that I've been to many places in the world and done some fantastic things, like working on mega-yachts, scuba diving, horse riding on beaches and in the bush, and managing safari camps at high-end lodges,' she says.

As a youngster she appeared happy-go-lucky. 'I was often the life and soul of the party but over my life I believe that my predominant mood has been one of sadness – a feeling that things are more difficult than they should be and that there was something missing, something elusive just out of reach. I avoided the pain of facing what I was truly feeling by chasing all those exciting trips and exotic lifestyles with lots of drinking and partying. My history clearly shows the patterns of constantly avoiding pain by chasing the next big thing.

'I became more cautious after my divorce, and found that more peace and quiet were a necessary refuge from the demands of the world and people. I've sobered in my 40s and I'm learning to channel my need to escape from life's hardships through inner work, like meditation instead of trips overseas. I've found true refuge in meditation and higher consciousness, and I continue to practise gratitude for that. For me, gratitude is the antidote to gluttony.

'I changed my language and use an inquiring approach to get to know people and situations more now, and I've been told that I come across as gentle and kind. I was probably quite selfish in my 20s.

'I've learned to appreciate more structure and caution, where it previously repelled me immediately. I'm a more compassionate, confident person now that I understand that it's okay to embrace both the light and the shadow within me. It's not arrogant to recognise and use my gifts.'

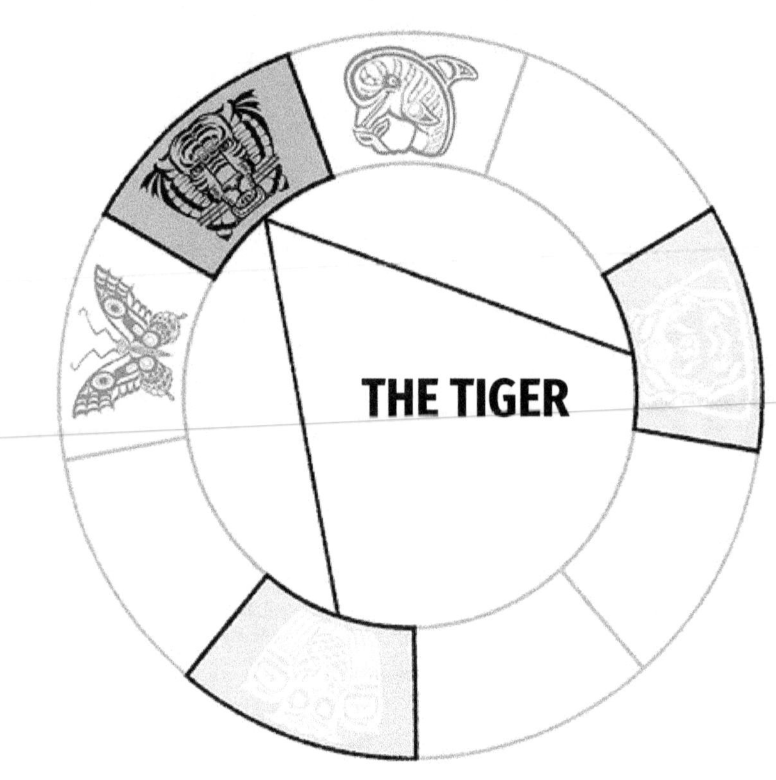

THE TIGER

'Just because the tiger prowls quietly doesn't mean it's intimidated.'

– Proverb.

Well-known Tigers

Donald Trump, Serena Williams, Queen Latifah, Susan Sarandon, Sean Connery, Martin Luther King Jnr, Frank Sinatra, Winston Churchill, Sean Penn, Dr Phil McGraw

Other names for the Tiger

The Active Controller, The Protector or The Challenger.

Are you a Tiger? Do you:

- Hide your vulnerability, your gentleness, since the story that plays out for you is that vulnerability is weakness whereas life favours the strong?
- Show determination to know the truth and pursue it relentlessly?
- Dislike ambiguity?
- Not flinch from conflict?
- Sometimes behave aggressively and insensitively to people around you?
- Appreciate people who take you on, and give as good as they get?
- Have a desire to make things right for the wronged of the world?

The Tiger is represented as type 8 in the enneagram.

Tigers are strong and courageous, with a hidden gentle giant. Independent, action-oriented, straight-talking and assertive, they have a great instinctual energy and are natural leaders – they're often founders of their own mega-corporations.

The Tiger is at home with conflict and willingly engages with contentious people or subjects. They're generally the people who step in and take charge of situations even when not asked for assistance. They fight for justice in a world where injustice is rife.

Although Tigers are quick to anger, because they're comfortable with the emotion, they can rapidly move through it. For non-Tigers, this sometimes makes for uncomfortable experiences, as some may be left licking their wounds, their injured pride leaving them less eager to forgive, forget and move on.

Self-determination is what Tigers value and pursue. They have a natural sense of self and their abilities, and because of their nothing-is-impossible attitude, they inspire people around them to take action, be brave, and show up as courageous.

For Tigers, being strong is the only way to be. Weak or soft emotions aren't available to them. They tend to ignore emotions like regret or guilt, and value anger and courage as strong emotions that bring change.

Triggers for The Tiger

- Being blindsided by people or events, or feeling duped or lied to.
- Believing there's been injustice.
- People who aren't direct or honest.
- When others don't take responsibility for their actions or behaviours.
- Being perceived as a bully because of their 'nothing gets in my way' attitude.
- The inaction or procrastination of others.

The Tiger's unconscious story: 'I can't be vulnerable'

The Tiger's story is that being weak and/or vulnerable would never be an option for them. Their unconscious decision is to be the person who growls first rather than being growled at.

Unfortunately, with their lust for life and control, they often fail to recognise their strength and the voracity with which they engage in life, and others can experience them as aggressive and combative.

The Tiger is bold in stature, dress sense, language and even emotion. Audacious, they don't hesitate to take charge of their lives and the lives of those who're important to them, and they take brave, decisive actions while masking their softness.

Cross them at your peril. Equally, don't be timid, unsure of yourself or lacking in confidence in the presence of a Tiger; they will eat you alive.

The need to mask their vulnerability makes it difficult for Tigers to show true emotions in relationships, thus often blocking their ability to connect with people or to love themselves from a heart-centred space.

The healthy Tiger

Mothers or moguls, ballerinas or businessmen, handymen or head honchos – roles don't define The Tiger. Tigers are simply a force to be reckoned with. They think big, talk big and act big. They naturally gravitate to positions that hold power and authority. Their lust for life enables them to tackle larger-than-life visions and tasks and, seemingly effortlessly, to move people and organisations forward.

The Tiger eschews unfairness. If they spot any form of it shown to a defenceless person, they'll take it on as their own battle, stepping in and sorting it out.

They can be generous to a fault towards the gentle-hearted. This softer, more innocent side of them is a selfless gift to the world.

Tigers value the truth. They will tell you something as it is and they expect others to do the same with them.

They have no qualms overriding someone's conversation mid-sentence or suggesting they're talking drivel. Usually, it's done without malice: it's simply their need to get to the bottom of things by the most direct route so that action can be taken to achieve the results they want.

The healthy Tiger has moved from a place of armouring to

de-armouring. They've recognised that disallowing space in their lives for more sensitive emotions hasn't served them, that the protection is unnecessary, and that their gentleness is appealing.

A healthy Tiger has the ability to slow down; to be considered in their approach, in their actions; to take time to reflect on the opinions of others; and to research a situation or even multiple scenarios before taking action.

The unhealthy Tiger: The Bull

Bulls move forcefully through the china shop of life, leaving broken people and relationships in their wake. They tend to use more force and more brute strength than needed. They stride forward, often steamrolling others or dragging them along with them.

A Bull will defy any attempt to be controlled and may become ruthless and dictatorial, with a might-makes-right attitude.

Bulls are known to rebel against all forms of authority, which can put them under substantial mental, physical and emotional pressure as they refuse to acknowledge their own limitations. They bellow their anger to the world by physical expression, such as uncontrolled sexual lust, verbal abuse or emotional mistreatment. When in this state, The Bull feels rejected by the world and lacks the capacity to trust anyone or anything other than themselves.

With these negative emotions left unattended, Bulls may develop delusions about their power and invincibility, which can lead to megalomania, feelings of omnipotence and invulnerability, and recklessness.

With their high energy and enthusiasm, Bulls tend to over-exert and over-consume, which creates an excessive style. In their Bullish state, they engage lustfully in everything that life has to offer, almost challenging the world to disprove their strength. Such overindulgence may be seen in overeating, excessive smoking and drinking, and working too hard, all while risking their health and ignoring warnings from their body or the people around them.

The Tiger at work

There are two very distinct views of the Tiger. In one, they're experienced as bullying, pushy, controlling and demanding. In the other, they're seen to be the champion, the provider, the protector, the captain who ensures that every last member of his crew and passengers are safe.

The Tiger is the top brass, the head honcho. Tigers are all about action, taking the initiative and making things happen. Successful motivators and leaders, Tigers inspire people with their confidence, capacity and lust for life.

Tigers are natural mentors, guiding people to greater competence personally and in what they do in the world. They may appear a little daunting and scary but getting past their roar is well worth the effort.

They have a formidable 'can-do' attitude to life. Nothing and no-one stops them performing the task at hand. They lack an off switch or pause button. They expect everyone to push forward, past their constraints. Employees or colleagues can feel drained by the energy needed to work alongside them.

Tigers often work an inordinate number of hours a week, and recognise that their body needs attention only when they're mentally, physically and emotionally spent. They live at a level of denial that means they push through the signals of wear and tear their bodies scream at them, and keep going even if extremely ill.

They're exceptionally direct and expect you, as a colleague, to be the same. They have no time for chitchat. They want to get to the point and move on.

One thing is sure when working with this personality type: you'll always know where you stand. If you have their respect, they'll fight tooth and nail for you, as they're fiercely protective of those they care about.

Tigers are quick to anger in any situation. But, importantly, they don't linger and stew in the emotion; anger for them is the emotion that brings healthy change. Once they've said what they need to say, they move on – you can expect a hug or high-five minutes later, with no hard feelings.

Tigers respect colleagues who fight back, who're able to meet them head-on.

The Tiger in relationships

For The Tiger parent, it's about survival of the fittest; they want their children to be able to face any adversity with absolute courage. They're very protective of those who they love and, in what might appear a paradox to some, can be remarkably gentle and nurturing. As much as they would be the Tiger Dad who tells their daughter to wipe away her tears, they'd be in the front row at that same daughter's ballet concert, wiping away their own tears of pride and joy.

Tigers are exceptionally guarded with their emotions.

As a partner, Tigers don't want to be controlled. They appreciate it when their partner is honest and direct with them, and that partner must understand that their harsh words are most often a deflection of their hurt and vulnerability, and not a personal attack.

A TIGER'S STORY: FROM THE STRONG CAME FORTH SWEETNESS

Ellie, a 33-year-old chief of staff, was in trouble at work: a number of her colleagues had lodged complaints of aggressive behaviour and intimidation by her.

She was hard on her colleagues, showing no empathy. One of the complainants mentioned that Ellie had found her crying in the bathroom, and told her to 'stop snivelling' and get back to her desk. Ellie hadn't asked why the colleague was upset; it was as if the sight of tears brought out the worst in her.

Another complaint was that she often raised her voice in anger in meeting rooms, especially when she thought women were deferring to their male counterparts. It seems that she saw this as a sign of weakness.

The daughter of a military man, Ellie had learned from an early age that there was no time or space for tears, that to be loved in the world she had to be tough and fight her own battles.

'Working with Juanene, I first had to understand what underpinned my actions, and then explore the impact of my behaviour not only on the people around me but on myself,' she says. 'Dropping my guard and being vulnerable in our sessions was incredibly difficult for me, and it took a concerted effort from me to show up for our sessions each month knowing how tough it was for me to speak about my childhood and the behaviours that I had learned as a form of survival.

'One of my proudest moments was when I overheard a new colleague describe me as the best example of a woman leader she'd experienced: gently powerful.'

Self-growth work

Possible areas of focus:
- Demonstrate vulnerability and innocence.
- Be compassionate towards yourself; welcome support.
- Take a more measured approach; slow down.
- Listen to more than your own voice.
- Experiment with a wider range of emotions

Slow down

Tigers are all about taking immediate action and control, so it's hard for them to slow down. They need to smell the coffee *and* the roses, to listen to others and to themselves. When they do slow down, they become more aware of their actions, more insightful, more discerning about who they are and whom they desire to be.

Self-check questions
How might I add downtime to my diary?
What's my current pace? Can I slow it down a notch (or two)?

Affirmations
I practise a slower pace in life so that I'm able to be more present.
I practise patience.

Soften up

Tigers need to learn to love everything about themselves, including their vulnerability and their weaknesses. They don't always have to wear a mask of toughness and invincibility.

Do heart-centred work

A big challenge for The Tiger is to recognise that emotional intelligence is as important as getting the task done. Hear and welcome others' perspectives without belittling or dismissing them. This work will support you in building a repertoire of emotions that you might otherwise label as weak, soft or gushy, and an ease in engaging with those emotions.

Lighten up

Tigers can be very intense and serious – they want to make the world a bigger, better place in the quickest, most efficient way. It's imperative that they lighten up, recharge their energy levels and let life take them on a little meander. Tigers have to work at relaxing a little, having fun and realising that not everything in life requires action and achievements. Go dancing, watch a comedy show, take acting classes, learn to salsa.

Self-check questions
How might I be less intense in my work relationships?
On a scale of 1 to 10, where are my energy levels really?

Affirmations
I'm making time for me.
I'm recharging and slowing down.

Step aside for others to lead

You don't always need to lead and support. Give others a turn. You have a wealth of knowledge, so how about creating a learning experience for yourself and those you mentor? In stepping back, you afford yourself an opportunity to be supported.

Self-check questions
How might I empower the people around me by taking a step back and giving them the space to make their own decisions?
If I ask for support, what might shift in the dynamics of the team?

Affirmations
I trust the decisions of my team.
I use my strength and power to assist others.

A TIGER'S STORY: FIGHTING FOR JUSTICE

Naz, a 44-year-old business partner in the financial sector, had much to deal with during the 2008 financial crisis: she was informed by her superiors that almost half the teams she worked with were to be notified of their immediate retrenchment.

The protector in her jumped into action: where other managers did little or nothing to help their people, Naz set up a meeting with her full team of about 60 people, and told them that she'd make it her business that each one of them find a new role in the organisation or in another company. For this to happen, she told them, she needed everyone's commitment to staying positive.

'I met individually with each person, spending time ensuring that their CVs were current and updated, asking what their ideal role was, and, if they had a choice, what organisation they'd ideally want to work for. Within four months, I'd found every retrenched person a new role within the organisation, or they'd been offered a role in another company, or they'd accepted a voluntary retrenchment package.'

Naz was adamant that not one of her people was going to be financially impacted, and no-one was. It was a mammoth task, one that took its toll on her – mentally, physically and emotionally. She pushed herself every day, working very long hours to ensure the security of her people. There were no weekends or off days for her during this time, even though everyone around her noticed her weight loss, her stifled yawn and her irritability.

As soon as the last person had been reassigned, Naz finally admitted to her exhaustion. She resigned from her job, cleared out all commitments in her diary and took herself off on a well-deserved mini-sabbatical.

Paths to greater success

Life lesson

To harness your life force in productive ways and to accept your vulnerability.

Emotional awareness practice

Notice how angry you are when you realise you've been blindsided by a trusted colleague, or how impatient you become when waiting for people to hurry along and get to the damn point of the conversation.

Step 1: Name the emotion

What are you feeling? Name the emotion.

Tigers might find this exercise – stepping into the domain of emotions – somewhat difficult. One of the first steps would be to notice where in their body they're feeling the emotion. Have they experienced it before? What is it asking of them?

Step 2: Find the story

What's the story you're telling about yourself, the situation or the other person?

- *That's a deliberate injustice.*
- *I feel blindsided.*
- *They're useless at what they do and they're slowing me down.*
- *The world has no time or space for the weak.*

Step 3: Reframe the story

If there was a neutral observer to this situation, what story might they tell? What's a different story that you're not seeing?

- *Is that what really happened?*
- *Am I jumping to my usual anger response without looking more*

deeply at what's actually going on?

- *What conversations need to happen between me and the team around delivery expectations?*
- *Is it true that being vulnerable is a sign of weakness?*

Physical awareness practice

Tigers are likely to be dissociated from their body. Any form of body work or slow exercise, like tai chi, yoga, pilates or even ballet, is of huge benefit. Take a walk in nature, a stroll along the beach barefoot. Be in the moment. Slow your breathing.

If you're open to it, how about trying a concept known as 'forest bathing'? It's the mindful practice of going into a forest and absorbing the atmosphere through touch, sight, scent, sound and taste.

Before you react to a situation, follow your breath down and tune in to what you're feeling and sensing inside. Do the breathing exercise recommended on page 29. This pause will help lessen the emotion and your reactivity, although it may bring up an unexpected sense of vulnerability. Its benefits are that it will increase your emotional receptivity and empathy, opening new possibilities in relationships. At the same time, having more emotional intelligence will make you a more effective leader.

Language awareness practice

Your language may sound like:

- ✗ *I'm telling you.*
- ✗ *Because I said so.*
- ✗ *Don't you dare.*
- ✗ *Are you going to war with me? You're going to lose.*

How about a new refrain?

✓ *Can I ask for your help, please?*
✓ *What are your thoughts on the matter?*
✓ *That would generally get me riled up but let me hear your side of the story.*
✓ *I'm not used to people challenging me, so I'm finding this tough right now.*

A TIGER'S STORY: I AM WOMAN — HEAR ME ROAR

'When I was 6 years old my mother told me that she was leaving my stepfather. She told me he'd been physically abusing her. She'd endured the abuse for my sake, to protect me, or so she thought,' says Sibongile, a 46-year-old CEO.

'When my mother told me about her decision I saw that her spirit was broken – but at the same I saw a fierce determination in her to start over and provide for me. That moment had a profound impact on my life. I promised myself, even as a little girl, that I'd work hard at school, pass my exams, have a good job and take care of my mother. I never wanted her to rely on a man to provide for her, nor did I want to be in her situation of being vulnerable.

'I became driven to do well academically and then in my career. My determination to succeed made people in my team see me as a slave driver at times. It's a trait that I try to guard against, but I can't say I'm always successful, especially when the pressure is on to deliver.

'Juanene helped me recognise the behavioural patterns that I repeated again and again in my life. I realised that I move swiftly and decisively on issues, leaving behind others in my team, especially those who may require more time to digest information before making a decision. They felt bullied into agreeing with me. Juanene suggested I confess to the team my tendency to speed ahead and my need for their help to remind me to slow down when required. It was a simple action but it had positive results.

'Another of the adjustments I made was my clothes. I used to wear dark-coloured formal suits and Juanene suggested that I could experiment with lighter colours or wear floral blouses or scarfs with my suits. When I did, people gave me such positive feedback. They found me to be more relatable and approachable.'

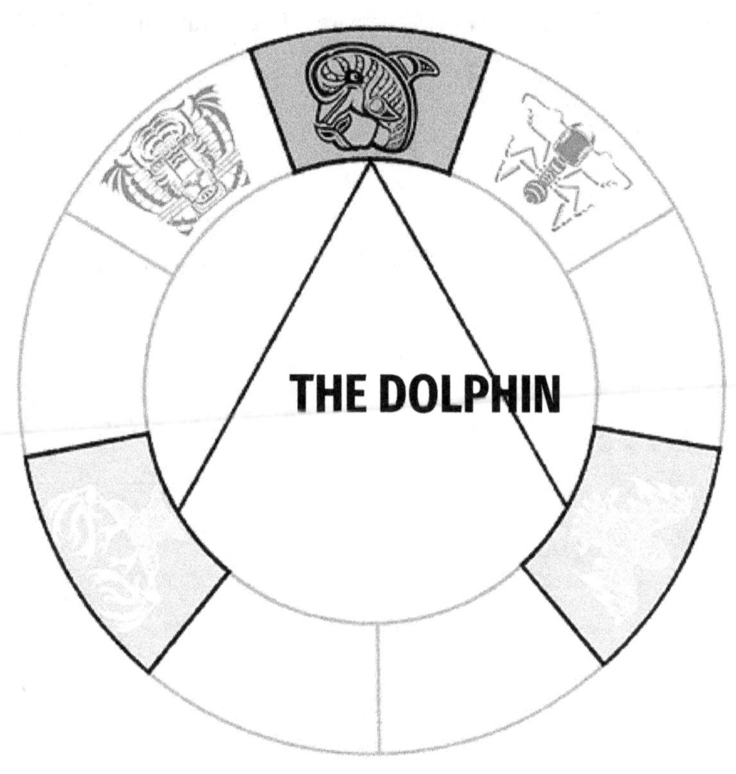

THE DOLPHIN

'A dolphin's smile is the greatest deception. It creates the
illusion that they're always happy.'
– Ric O'Barry

Well-known Dolphins

Whoopi Goldberg, Morgan Freeman, Walt Disney, Sophia Loren,
Kevin Costner, Ronald Reagan, Janet Jackson, Toby McGuire.

Other names for the Dolphin

The Peacemaker, The Mediator or The Facilitator.

Are you a Dolphin? Do you:
- Forget your own needs and desires?
- Pride yourself on being agreeable and keeping the peace?
- Battle with indecision?
- Feel it important that people get along, that they listen to each other, that there's shared and mutual respect?
- Function best in familiar patterns in your life?
- Have a lukewarm emotional intensity?
- Experience people taking advantage of your appeasing nature?

The Dolphin is represented as type 9 in the enneagram.

Easygoing, passive and indirect in communication, Dolphins
are the peacemakers and mediators of the world. This doesn't mean
peace and harmony for themselves, however. On the contrary,
Dolphins are often in conflict with themselves, saying yes when
they want to say no, just to avoid conflict. They're known to put
their own needs and desires so far out of mind that they somehow
forget that they have dreams of their own.

The Dolphin can also 'merge' with a significant other – a
business or romantic partner or a family friend – and in the process
give up their own desires in favour of the other.

Dolphins are sensitive to being ignored or having their opinion dismissed. This then plays out like a self-fulfilling prophecy: they don't say what they want to say, so people tend to forget they're there, so they aren't asked for their view, and as a result they retreat even further into their own world.

Dolphins are slow to show anger but this doesn't mean they don't feel it. Their stifled irritation may show up as stubbornness or passive-aggressive behaviour. They can suppress their anger, perhaps for decades, but when it suddenly erupts, it creates the very turmoil they're trying to avoid.

Triggers for The Dolphin

- Feeling they're being told or directed to do something that may potentially cause turmoil for themselves or others.
- Not being seen or heard.
- Being in a space of others complaining.
- Any situation involving conflict.
- When anger is directed at them.
- Feeling angry and not knowing how to manage it.

The Dolphin's unconscious story: 'I can't be controlled. I can't be in turmoil'

Dolphins live life as if their sole purpose is to maintain harmony. They tend not to make decisions that may negatively impact others, and may even procrastinate on a decision to such a degree that either someone else makes it for them or it's no longer necessary to decide at all.

Most Dolphins are self-effacing, focusing on the agenda of the other – not in the same way The Labrador would, which is more about 'I'll love you so that you love me', but rather 'I give up on my own needs so that I can support yours, and in that way I avoid conflict'.

Dolphins can be somewhat lazy about taking care of themselves, whether physically, mentally or emotionally. Their thinking is that they're better off ensuring that everyone else is alright, so as to sidestep any conflict. This self-forgetting trait is deeply ingrained.

Dolphins are exceptionally lovable, relaxed and easy to be with. They're adored because they're so low maintenance. Yet any Dolphin can tell you that it takes a lot of energy to project that serene exterior to keep the peace.

The healthy Dolphin

The Dolphin personality is warm, peace-loving, exceptionally supportive and trusting. Dolphins are innocent, simple, patient, unpretentious, good-natured and genuinely nice people. They're the ideal friends: they'll support rather than challenge you.

It's when they make themselves a priority and get their stuff together that they're the most formidable of people and make inspirational leaders. When head, heart and hand (thinking, feeling and action) are connected, Dolphins are as solid as a rock.

Dolphins have an innate way of determining the common purpose in a group or conversation, giving people around them the space for alignment, creating cohesion rather than division on a project. They have an uncanny way of seeing not only the big picture but, more importantly, how each individual fits into it. They appreciate how the whole is made up of individual parts. In the work environment, people feel safe in the knowledge that they're being led by someone who listens deeply to both client and employee.

Dolphins' view of the world is of peace. They're known to be optimistic and reassuring, and can have a healing, calming influence. They're great mediators and are often the glue that holds a group together. Not surprisingly, they excel at being diplomatic in any situation.

Dolphins generally don't own up to their own accomplishments and strengths, but when they're centred within themselves they can have the most enlightened understanding of every other personality type, and deep compassion for them.

When present to themselves, Dolphins become engaging,

dynamic and proactive as they assert themselves in the world. In this state, they can manage their own dreams and desires in a healthy proportion to supporting the aspirations of others.

The unhealthy Dolphin: The Elephant

The Elephant can be passive-aggressive and stubborn. Because they say yes when they mean no, in the pursuit of avoiding conflict, they may silently fume, not do the job, procrastinate, withdraw or become sullen. They may ignore requests or deadlines and potentially spoil a project.

Solid and unmoving, The Elephant can stay in a job or marriage long after its sell-by date because it enables them to avoid any potential conflict and turmoil, and they've told themselves that it's more comfortable being in the space than out of it.

Elephants battle to be direct and will seldom correct or confront people even if the other person is at fault. They tend to be neutral and not offer up an opinion. In this state, Elephants can be tripped up by their diplomacy, so careful in choosing their words and in their delivery that they don't convey a clear, concise message. The recipient is none the wiser about the true and tough message.

Elephants can become highly repressed, and in this state of arrested development ultimately become ineffectual. They may feel incapable of facing problems and can wilfully separate themselves from all conflict, to the extent that they neglect their own needs.

Elephants may feel deeply hurt at having their needs unsatisfied but rather than speaking out about this, will amp up the levels of people-pleasing to mask the pain inside.

The Dolphin at work

Dolphins are able to facilitate genuine, deeply shared under-standing between diverse team members as they seek common ground. They seek group consensus before taking actions that will impact everyone.

Affable, friendly and witty, they're able to lighten the most serious of moods and situations. Paradoxically, however, they also want to be taken seriously; and while their tendency is to stay in the background, they also want to be acknowledged. Because they often don't assert themselves, people forget they're there, and this risks their valid viewpoints being completely discounted.

As leaders, Dolphins tend to lead from the background or the sides, not front and centre. They lead from a space where every voice matters. The ever-present guide, you can talk to The Dolphin about anything and they'll never get angry; they listen so intently that you feel heard, every time.

Dolphins appear to be uncomplicated, and people love them for that, but it's not entirely the reality. They can become passive-aggressive or stubborn, or 'forget' to do something you've asked them because they didn't want to do it in the first place but avoided telling you so because it might have created conflict.

When Dolphins are in tune with their own strengths, they make the most successful leaders, able to move mountains because of their innate listening, deep caring and mediating skills. They also then have the capacity to manage their anger positively, and this is a good thing as it communicates the need of 'this thing has to change'.

I recently observed a Dolphin allow each of the 24 people present in a room to contribute to the conversation. Each time he was asked if he had anything to add, he answered no. Finally, the facilitator forgot to return to him and closed the conversation. Dolphins fall asleep on themselves; after time, so do others.

The Dolphin in relationships

As parents, Dolphins are relaxed, loving, supportive and accepting of their children. In their need to be the accommodating parent, however, they might be too soft, and not offer appropriate boundaries and guidance for their kids, deferring this aspect of parenting to the other parent.

As partners, Dolphins avoid conflict and would rather give up on their own desires to support the other person's. For example, if their partner suggests going out for Thai food, the Dolphin will agree. They might not particularly feel like Thai food or they may be exhausted and really want to eat at home, but rather than rock the boat and create conflict or suggest something different, they agree so as to please.

They're known to be passive-aggressive, holding onto their emotions and opinions instead of risking conflict in their relationships.

A DOLPHIN'S STORY: 'EVEN I FEARED THE DRAGON'

Bob was in his late 60s when his wife of fifty years died. It was only after this that he was able to admit that while she'd been 'an absolute sweetheart' in the early days of their courting and marriage, after they'd hit a rough financial patch and she'd had to go to work, she'd changed from 'my sweet girl to the dragon lady'.

Bob learned very quickly to keep the peace at home for the sake of the children: it was far easier for him to agree with whatever it was that she wanted. 'When she wanted to travel to India with the three kids, we went even though I had no desire to go there. When she wanted a new car, even though her car was only eighteen months old, I got her one. When she asked for separate bedrooms, I agreed even though it wasn't what I wanted.'

Bob discovered late in his life how 'forgetting' about his needs had played out. 'Who am I now with her no longer here? I've forgotten what I like and what I don't like. I've spent half a century agreeing to stuff just to keep the peace. It feels like I'm starting my adult life again, only just discovering myself.'

Self-growth work

Possible areas of focus:
- Becoming present for yourself.
- Knowing what you do and don't want.
- Taking back your personal power.
- Knowing that conflict is part of life.
- Asking for what you want.

Take a stand

The core challenge for the Dolphin is to take a stand for what they truly desire. Being the supreme democrat, listening to a multitude of voices and perspectives, they lose sight of what they want or of their stance. What should be totally acceptable and required of them is to focus on their agenda, ask for what they want, and disagree if they have a different opinion.

Self-check questions
What's important to me and what's the next right action for me to take?
How do I bring my disagreement to this conversation?

Affirmations
I focus on my own agenda.
I take care of my own needs.

Determine your own goals

Focus on your own goals, not the goals of others. Determine a goal, map out how you're going to get there, and determine what possible bumps in the road may appear, like procrastinating or telling yourself it's no longer important.

Speak up, make your voice heard

Bring your voice into the conversation. Ask for what you want. Be more direct. Say no if that's what you feel. Correct others when they get it wrong.

Rock the boat

Life isn't about always keeping the peace. From time to time it's necessary to instigate disorder, for how else do we bring about change?

Be active

Many Dolphins are out of touch with their bodies. They can become sloth-like in their ways, comfort-eating too much or drinking excessively in an effort to numb their pain. They can also be physically idle and would rather binge-watch a TV series than go for a walk.

A DOLPHIN'S STORY: SAYING WHAT YOU WANT

Antoine, a 30-year-old hotelier at the time he and I began our coaching engagement, spoke of his profession as being in his blood: he'd grown up in his grandparents' hotel and it was a natural assumption by his family that he would take over the running of the hotel when his parents retired.

But he came to realise that he didn't want to be involved in the hospitality industry after all, and he definitely didn't want to be the next manager of the family hotel. What he wanted to do was make wine.

'I worked with Juanene for about eight months. It was tough. She was tough. I'd send her an email every few weeks, trying to get out of the contract, because that appeared easier at the time than my having to face my parents with the news that I didn't want to take over the running of our family hotel. Thank heavens she held me accountable to the coaching. I was able to state with clarity what it was that I wanted, and for me to stand up for me and my dreams and desires.'

Antoine finally followed his own dream, studying winemaking, and during this period of his life he lost almost 20 kg of excess weight. 'I felt that I'd finally put down the rock I'd been carrying around for fifteen years, from the day my parents had told me as a teen that my future was the hotel.'

Paths to greater success

Life lesson

To reclaim yourself and wake up to your own personal priorities.

Emotional awareness practice

Awareness might mean noticing how you stifle your anger, and become passive-aggressive or compliant, instead of disagreeing with a prevailing sentiment or challenging a conversation.

Step 1: Name the emotion

What are you really feeling? Name the emotion.

Own your anger. Recognise that you're holding resentment in your body.

Step 2: Find the story

What's the story you're telling about yourself, the situation or the other person?

- *I've been ignored and overlooked; no one considers my point of view.*
- *It's impossible for me to show my anger.*
- *It's not important for me to be the centre of attention.*

Step 3: Reframe the story

What story might a neutral observer to this situation tell? What's a different story that you're not seeing?

- *Where do I go quiet and then blame others for ignoring me?*
- *What would happen if I said I was angry?*
- *What do I think would happen if I took centre stage?*

Physical awareness practice

It's a great practice for a Dolphin to look in the mirror regularly and work at truly seeing themselves. Practise standing or moving in a more commanding fashion. Practise speaking more assertively.

Because Dolphins internalise anger, it's also a healthy practice for them to become aware of where they hold anger in their bodies. They may even become aware of an accelerated heart rate.

More than most other personality types, Dolphins need to focus on breathing into the chest, not belly breathing. Chest breaths are more elevating and help energy to rise. Do the breathing exercise recommended on page 29.

Language awareness practice

Language for a Dolphin may sound something like:

- ✗ *It's just easier to say yes and keep the peace.*
- ✗ *I can't bear being around anger and conflict situations.*
- ✗ *I don't know what goals I have.*
- ✗ *It doesn't matter that my voice wasn't heard in the meeting.*

How about a new refrain?

- ✓ *What's the impact on me of always keeping the peace?*
- ✓ *Is it possible that being around anger and conflict is triggering me because I avoid it myself?*
- ✓ *What's preventing me from saying no?*
- ✓ *What if I say what I need to say at the beginning of the meeting tomorrow morning?*

A DOLPHIN'S STORY: KEEPING THE PEACE

Sashi, a 45-year-old senior manager, describes herself as patient and calm. 'I go with the natural rhythm of the environment. I'm authentic in every way. What you see is what you get, and I always keep my promises.'

But there's one thing she detests: being micro-managed. 'If I feel stifled or that someone is watching over me continually, I believe that they think me incompetent. I want to be independent and I want to feel that I'm contributing to something valuable.

'I came to realise in working with Juanene that the reason this happened was that I didn't bring my opinion or perspective into a meeting. I didn't push back. I agreed to timelines and project outcomes that I knew wouldn't work, and then I'd spend time at my desk complaining about the manager and how the project was a complete waste of my time.

'I believe in balance in life, and that you need to be harmonious at home and work,' she says, explaining that she tends to step into the mediator shoes in any situation she finds conflictual. 'I want to sort it out. I believe I'm very good at being fair to all parties and being honest about what I believe to be the best solution to regain harmony. If I need to make a sacrifice for this to happen, I will.

'I've definitely become more assertive in my personal relationship. I know now that having a harmonious environment isn't required all the time. I speak my mind more now. I think my husband was shocked at the start but he's got used to it. I can be very feisty.'

Tips on relating to the other animal types

Reading through the animal types, you may identify the traits of a friend, family member or colleague, and have a proverbial 'aha!' moment in uncovering a greater sense of understanding of why they do what they do. That, in turn, will enable you to empathise with them and to approach them, and perhaps the conversation, in a new way. It could just be that one thing that allows you to work more cohesively together.

Tips on relating to Ants

- Remember that even though they're critical, Ants are hypersensitive to criticism of themselves.
- Respect their integrity. Try to avoid making agreements that you may not keep, neglecting proper procedures or not having good manners.
- Challenge them to see more than one right way forward.
- Remind them to temper their judgement with fairness and forgiveness, and encourage them to allow other resolutions.

Tips on relating to Labradors

- Be gentle when you criticise Labradors: criticism makes them feel unworthy of your love.
- Do something for them without them having done anything for you.
- Acknowledge them with a kind or generous word.
- Talk about the value they bring to the world in general and your world in particular.

Tips on relating to Eagles

- Let Eagles know you care for who they are, more than what they accomplish.
- Support them in speaking about their emotions and possibly demonstrating this by you speaking about your feelings.
- Know they're impatient.
- Demonstrate with your actions that you understand their fast-paced and achievement-focused world.

Tips on relating to Black Stallions

- Appreciate Black Stallions' emotional intensity, creativity and individualism.
- When they're upset, don't take everything they say too literally – they're known to overdramatise an event.
- Acknowledge their feeling of what's missing and at the same time show them what they have.
- Black Stallions love to offload their emotions. Allow them to speak without interrupting, then help them gain a different perspective, perhaps asking them how else the situation may be viewed.

Tips on relating to Owls

- Know that they're not rejecting you when they demand their privacy.
- Don't badger them for them to speak about their feelings. Rather create a safe space for them to do this in their own time.
- Don't put them on the spot and pressurise them for a quick answer or decision; give them sufficient time to consider the request,
- Be curious when engaging with them: don't make assumptions about what's happening in their lives.

Tips on relating to Deers

- Be trustworthy and ensure consistency in your engagements with them.
- Be willing to engage in conversations about what could go wrong before you can move into what's right.
- Be upfront. Tell the truth. Don't be ambiguous.
- Disclose your own concerns.

Tips on relating to Butterflies

- Join Butterflies in having fun and exploring new possibilities.
- Show your appreciation for their positivity.
- Be specific in what you need or want from them.
- Create the space for them to speak of painful memories or about their sadness.

Tips on relating to Tigers

- Hold your ground when dealing with Tigers. Don't buckle under their bullying tendencies.
- Be direct yet empathetic in your engagement with them.
- Recognise their need for autonomy; don't try to cage them in.
- Challenge them to be open to others' perspectives and to what else is out there.

Tips on relating to Dolphins

- Allow them the space to express their anger.
- Encourage them to engage in some form of exercise.
- If you sense their indecision, ask them if they need more time, or if they'd like to consider another action or approach.
- Support them in determining their own goals and then taking action.

Acknowledgements

To my daughters, Geneviève and Ariane: may you have the courage to tame your inner stories and manifest the authentic richness that is you.

To Philippe, thank you for your constant and unwavering belief in and support of me.

To my incredible clients, thank you for giving me the space to practise one of my greatest loves and for contributing to my personal growth.

To Kate and Sarah, thank you for your guidance and encouragement, and for pushing me over the line.

Thank you to the people who offered encouragement and expertise along the way, Clare, Neville, Robert, Sandy, Ilana.

To the beta-readers who took time to give tough, professional feedback on the rudimentary bones of a passion project.

To the enneagram teachers in my life – Beatrice Chestnut, Dirk Cloete, Lucille Greeff, Uranio Paes and every enneagram author whose books I've devoured: thank you for unlocking the depth of me.

To the facilitators who've enabled me in taking this training to the world, thank you for sharing your passion and knowledge with me.

And to my editor Tracey Hawthorne, who agreed to partner with me, a first time author – thank you for your patience, your support and care.

References

Chapman, G. 1992. *The 5 Love Languages: How to Express Heartfelt Commitment to Your Mate*. Illinois, USA: Northfield Publishing.

Chestnut, B. 2017. *The Nine Types of Leadership: Mastering the Art of People in the 21st-Century Workplace*. USA: Post Hill Press.

Chestnut, B. 2013. *The Complete Enneagram 27 Paths to Greater Self – Knowledge*. USA: She Writes Press.

Heuertz, C. 2017. *The Sacred Enneagram*. USA: HarperCollins.

Hurley, K. and Dobson, T. 1991. *What's My Type?* USA: HarperCollins.

Lapid-Bogda, G. 2004. *Bringing Out the Best in Yourself at Work*. Blacklick, USA: McGraw-Hill Professional Publishing.

Maitri, S. 2001. *The Spiritual Dimension of the Enneagram*. USA: Penguin Putnam.

Perlmutter, D and Villoldo, Alberto. 2012. *Power Up Your Brain: The Neuroscience of Enlightenment*. California, USA: Hay House.

Riso, D. and Hudson, R. 1999. *The Wisdom of The Enneagram*. New York: Bantam Books.

Ruiz, DM. 2018. *The Four Agreements: A Practical Guide to Personal Freedom*. California, USA: Amber-Allen Publishing, Incorporated.

The Narrative Enneagram. https://enneagramworldwide.com/